DELICIOUS

Chilango

TOP 10

HEALTHIEST
HIGH STREET CHAINS

BEST
BURRITO
I EVER HAD

THE *Chilango*
BURRITO
BIBLE

MIND-BLOWING
MEXICAN FLAVOURS

ERIC PARTAKER & DAN HOUGHTON

sphere

First published in Great Britain in 2019 by Sphere

A CIP catalogue record for this book is available from the British
Library.

ISBN 978-0-7515-7353-4

Printed and bound in China

10 9 8 7 6 5 4 3 2 1

Book creation and design by Harris + Wilson Ltd

Managing Editor: Judy Barratt
Art Director: Manisha Patel
Recipe Consultants: Mark Miller, Stefan Cosser and Dan Booth
Home Economist: Nicola Graimes
Commissioned Photographer: Dave Brown @ Ape Inc.
Food Stylist: Rebecca Woods

Sphere
An imprint of
Little, Brown Book Group, Carmelite House,
50 Victoria Embankment, London EC4Y 0DZ

An Hachette UK Company
www.hachette.co.uk
www.littlebrown.co.uk

NOTES ON THE RECIPES
Unless otherwise specified, use:
Medium free-range or organic eggs
Fresh herbs
Medium-sized vegetables
Full-fat dairy products
Unwaxed citrus fruits
Organic, free-range meat
Fish from sustainable sources

Oven temperatures are for a conventional oven. If using a fan
oven, reduce the given temperature by 20°C.

Shop-bought sauces, condiments and jams may include allergens.
Please always check the labels – and all your ingredients – before
using if you are cooking for someone with allergies.

All the information in this book is correct to the best of our
knowledge. If there are any errors or omissions, we will, if notified,
make corrections in any future editions.

Papers used by Sphere are from well-managed
forests and other responsible sources.

CONTENTS

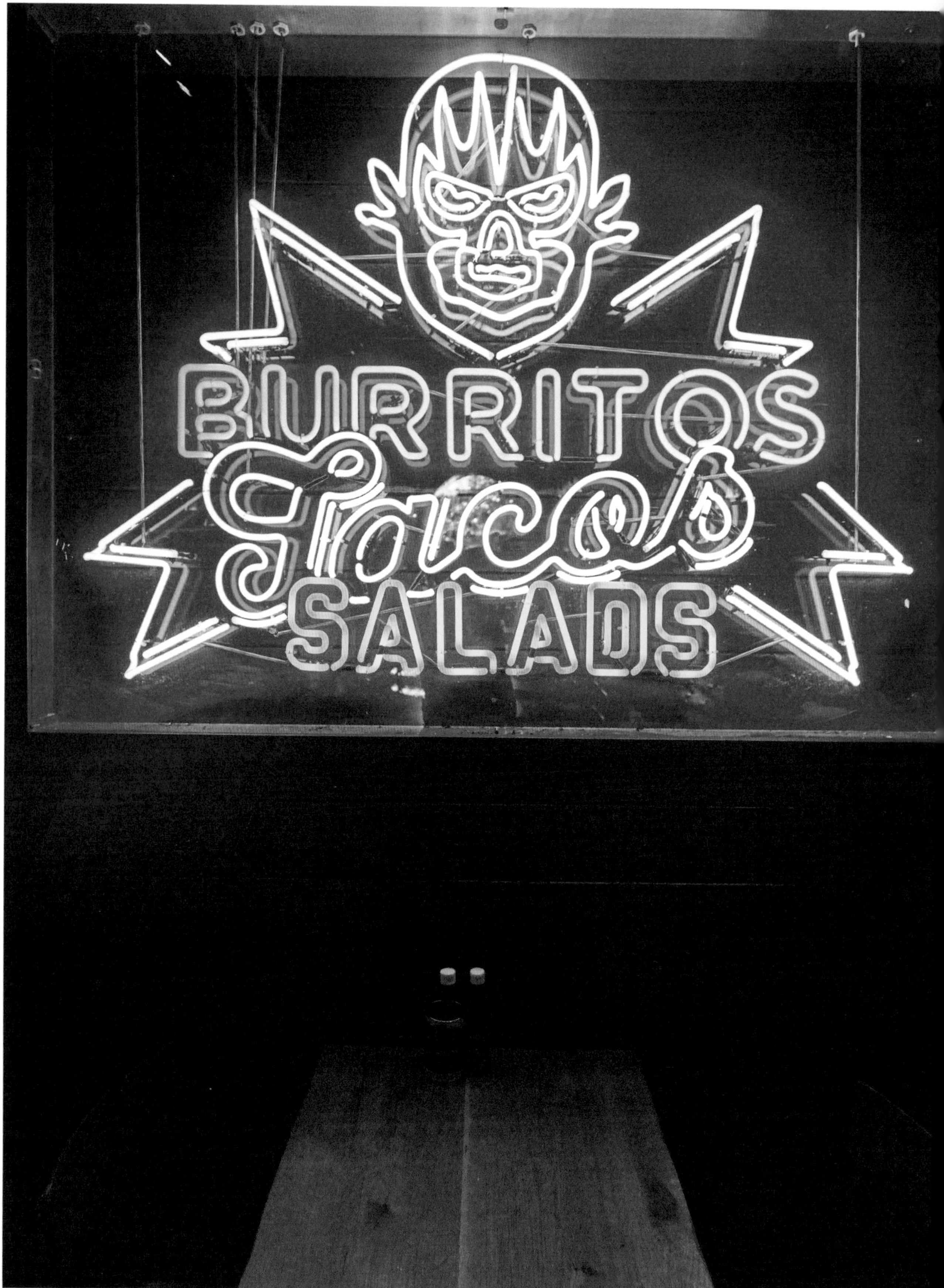
BURRITOS
Tacos
SALADS

FOREWORD

What you'll find in this book is something quite personal. At Chilango, we're not slaves to tradition. We're constantly experimenting and trying out new things – God only knows what stampede of flavours we'll wrap in a tortilla and serve up next. And that's the way we've approached our book. Mind-blowing Mexican, in a tortilla, at home.

Among the eighty-or-more recipes in this book, you'll find some you'll recognize straight from our restaurants, some that come pretty close, but give a twist here or there (well, we don't want to give away all our secrets), and many, many, many more burritos that are completely new. All thanks to the decade of experimenting that sits behind the brand, and the countless hours we spent in the kitchen, tasting, debating and tweaking all the recipes that follow.

You'll not only find Mexican burritos in the pages to come, but international burritos, too. These worldly wise offerings take that soft, warm tortilla and fill it with some of our favourite flavour combinations from around the globe. Which brings me onto something else. Let's talk authenticity.

I really couldn't give a shit about authenticity. Sorry, but it's the truth. This is not "authentic" Mexican food; it is Mexican-inspired. That means that in this book you won't find burritos the way they do them in Mexico. But who cares? That's not the point. We pay homage to flavour. Flavour is God. Mexico is a Saint.

One last thing – eating burritos will probably be messy. If that bothers you, you should probably return the book, or eat your burritos while wearing a hair net and hanging upside down. Or, just eat the damn burritos and stop being a pussy.

Enjoy!

Eric Partaker, Chilango Co-founder

THE CHILANGO STORY

DAN & ERIC, TWO MEXICAN FOOD ADDICTS

...DECIDE TO LEAVE SKYPE

2 YEARS OF CULINARY TOURS

...TO FIND THE BEST FLAVOURS & INGREDIENTS

COUNTLESS HOURS IN THE KITCHEN

2007 OPEN FIRST CHILANGO!

Chilango

VOTED NO. 1 MEXICAN RESTAURANT

WORLD DOMINATION BEGINS...

UNCOMMON ORIGINS

FROM SKYPE TO MEXICAN FOOD

If someone had told me twenty years ago, "Eric, one day you'll write a Mexican cookbook", I would have thought they were completely nuts. But here we are. So how the hell did this all happen?

1994. That's when my hot and sexy love affair with Mexican food began, when I started studying at the University of Illinois at Urbana-Champaign. During those next five years, I wolfed down countless burritos at the local Mexican restaurant on campus, La Bamba, after a night out. I seriously couldn't get enough of them. I loved eating burritos so much that I even entered burrito-eating competitions every year, using the prize money to help fund my spring break trips down to Florida, where I ate more burritos.

Soon after graduating, I left the US and the glory days of burrito-eating were over. I mean literally over, because there wasn't a single good Mexican place anywhere in sight.

THEN THINGS STARTED TO CHANGE

After a bit of consulting and non-profit work, and certainly nothing food-related, I ended up joining Skype in their London office. I was quickly paired up with Dan Houghton, the man who would become Chilango's co-founder, and we formed a sort of two-person team. The environment at Skype was electric, and it didn't take long for Dan and me to get the entrepreneurial bug ourselves. And so, on the back of a simple handshake, we made a pact: we'd leave Skype and start our own business, based on whatever idea one of us came up with first. Needless to say my Mexican food cravings got the better of me and we agreed to jump ship for warmer, Latin shores.

Believe it or not, Skype ended up being the perfect training ground for creating Chilango. During our two years there, we received a masterclass in product quality and branding. Skype succeeded where others didn't because the call quality and the software were vastly

superior to the competition. Similarly, everything was wrapped in a brand that people loved.

Those two core tenets – product quality and passionate branding – would form the bedrock of Chilango. Product quality, in that our flavours had to be out of this world; and passionate branding, in that people needed to passionately love what we stood for.

GETTING THE QUALITY RIGHT: FOOD DJS

We don't claim to be chefs, and never will. We're more like food DJs.

DJs are not necessarily the creators of the music they play. But they know what goes together, what sounds great in combination and what literally makes music to the ears. And that's our approach to food. As food DJs, we mix flavour combinations and culinary tracks that will make music to the taste buds. Or, as one of our guests put it best, that create a stampede of flavour.

Armed with our DJ perspective, our view was that all of the vibrant recipes we needed already existed in the world. We simply had to connect up the dots and find them. So we spent two years doing exactly that.

Amazing. Deeply satisfying. Mind blowing. Fresh and bursting with flavour. Food that makes you happy. Those were some of the very first things we said about our food, and those statements served as a filter for everything we tasted on the journey to where we are now.

As Flavour Hunters we ate our way through Mexico, as well as some of the largest Mexican communities in the US. Along the way we picked up recipes from both street vendors and high-end chefs. We left no stone unturned. We once even placed an ad offering $500 for a slow-cooked pork recipe. One of the many replies came from a chef from Cleveland, Ohio. I hopped on a plane. He picked me up from the airport. I tasted the pork recipe. It was amazing, just as he promised it would be. I handed him $500 in cash. Then he handed over the recipe, drove me back to the airport and I flew back to London. Later that evening we made the pork in one of our kitchens, and started serving it the next day. That was the pork sorted.

But it's not just recipe hunting that drives us, we do ingredient hunting as well. Certain ingredients you just have to source directly from Mexico, like the dried chillies that go into our marinades. So while in Mexico we held a press conference within a major farming community, shook hands with a few folks and thereafter had a great supply of chillies and other ingredients grown for us and then shipped directly to London.

Last but not least we're lucky to have some true artists as friends of the business – genuinely world-class culinary talent who have helped us along the way. For example, Michelin-starred chef Nuno Mendes went through our entire menu early on, adding bits of magic where we needed it. Stefan Cosser, the former Senior Development Chef at The Fat Duck, to this day helps us continuously improve. And Mark Miller, a celebrity chef in the US and the author of twelve cookbooks of his own, was absolutely instrumental in turning the *Chilango Burrito Bible* from dream to reality.

All the flavour hunting and food DJing seems to be working, with a long string of accolades and awards from the likes of *Zagat*, *Evening Standard*, *Grazia*, *Esquire*, *Time Out*, and *Harden*'s to name a few.

DEFINING THE BRAND: VIBRANCY

At Chilango our religion is *vibrancy*. Enjoying life to the fullest. Whether that's an everyday lunch or some big dream you have in mind, the way we look at it, you might as well go big and squeeze every last drop out of what the world has to offer.

With vibrancy making up our DNA, our menu development and flavours remain bold and strong, our restaurant interiors remain colourful and loud, and the personalities of our crew remain off-beat and fun. It is one simple word, but it really is our guiding force.

One of my favourite things that we do is ask candidates during the recruitment process to bring in their favourite t-shirt. During the interview we ask them to show us their shirt and explain why it's their favourite.

And that's often when the vibrancy happens.

One in ten interviewees will perhaps tell a super-engaging story behind the shirt. Or, the shirt itself may be the picture that screams a thousand vibrant words. Or, sometimes the person will even belt out a song related to the shirt. My favourite interview ever was a guy who unzipped his jacket during our chat to reveal a t-shirt that said "I didn't have a favourite t-shirt, so I got this one made."

I'll never forget that moment. "Holy Shit. Awesome. You're Hired," I said.

So there you have it. Chilango in a single word. *Vibrancy*. And it's the combination of our vibrant flavours, attitudes and experiences that create that oasis of happiness people have come to love and crave. I certainly hope you get a sense of that vibrancy as you try out some of the recipes in this book.

HOW TO USE THIS BOOK

As we're sure you gathered from the title, this book is mainly about burritos. There are some other things in here, too, so don't freak out. But it's mainly about burritos.

The thing about burritos (as well as tacos, fajitas and even bowls) is that they're built up in layers. (Almost) every dish in the book is a combination of different recipe flavours to set your taste buds alight. We've organized the book to make it as easy as possible for you to build your burritos just the way you want them – with some suggested combos to get you started.

PART ONE: THE BASICS

As a musical idol once said, let's start at the very beginning because it's a very good place to start. When it comes to burritos, the basics are the beginning. In this part of the book, you'll learn everything you need to know to understand how burritos work. We start with an explanation of what a burrito is, then how to roll one (don't skip this section – we promise you, you'll regret it if you do), as well as learning about all the chillies we use in the book and some of the basic cooking techniques you'll need to make sure you get the flavours just right.

PART TWO: THE EXTRAS

Rice and beans, cremas, salsas, salads, slaws and guacamoles – the crowd that cheers on the main act up on stage. Without them there is little point in having the concert at all and your burritos (and other meals in the book) are not complete.

PART THREE: THE BURRITOS (& FRIENDS)

Subdivided by filling type (Chicken, Beef, Pork, Veggie and Breakfast), this part is the meat of the book and mostly the meat of your burrito. Although, of course, we're not just thunderous meatheads – veggie fillings feature, too. And, like we say, it's not all about burritos.

For each burrito, fajita and taco recipe, there is a handy list of fillings from Part Two, and elsewhere in the book, that we believe deliver an awesome flavour combo. In fact, the recipes are built for flavour, so if you can go for the gold and include everything as suggested, your taste buds will thank you. But, then, we're not precious (much). Burritos are super-flexible by design. So you're free to swap things around or omit anything you don't like. Not hot on dairy? Leave it out. Love the sound of a particular burrito recipe, but worried about the heat-level? Swap out the spicy salsa with a mild one. Mixing and matching is all to the good.

You can even forget the burrito altogether (did we just say that?). If you're trying to cut down on gluten, just make the burrito recipe and place the ingredients in a bowl, instead of a tortilla. Fine with gluten, but want less carb? Keep the tortilla, but skip the rice.

PART FOUR: THE DESSERTS

Okay, we know that desserts aren't what you usually think of when you think of a burrito, or even Chilango. But we couldn't do a book on Mexican food without including s'murros (s'mores made with churros... oh, yes), and Lizzy from Marketing created a to-die-for dessert burrito that it would be rude not to share with the world. So here they are, and more. (Our editor thought this should be a section in Part Three, but we disagreed and – frankly – it's our book. Desserts need space of their own.)

Finally, at the end of the book we've given you a handy table that summarizes all the combos, recipe by recipe, in one place. You may never need it, but if you do (and, my goodness, we did when we were doing the photoshoots), you're welcome.

And that's it. What could be simpler?

PART ONE

THE BASICS

WHAT IS A BURRITO?

To me, a burrito is a blank canvas upon which you can paint anything you like. Or, more literally, it's a tortilla into which you can put whatever food makes you feel good and then wrap it up in a parcel to eat. Just about anything you can dream up can become a burrito. There are no rules. Burritos are simply magical.

Over the pages you'll find burritos that are savoury and burritos that are sweet; those that are dry and those that are wet (who can resist lathering a burrito in melted cheese and salsa); and even those that are gourmet – you gotta check out the Wagyu beef and lobster-tail Ultimate Surf 'n' Turf burrito on pages 110–11. All these are wrapped up in a tortilla from top to toe. Now, rolling a burrito is an art – but it is one that you can master, you just have to follow our handy guide over the following pages.

BURRITO VS TACO

A taco is a small, filled tortilla, served open and scooped up in the hand without wrapping or rolling. Traditionally, the taco tortilla is more likely to be made with corn than wheat flour, although we think you can use either. Whereas a single burrito is a meal in itself, you'll probably need two or more likely three tacos to come anywhere close to feeling like you've had something substantial to eat. Tacos tend to have a single filling topped with salsas and are particularly good for flavours that are a bit more delicate. Because they tend to be less laden than burritos, the flavours of the main event can shine through.

BURRITO VS FAJITA

Fajitas usually don't include rice and beans, so are a bit lighter. Use a large wheat tortilla for a fajita, which is made using a specific spice mix to coat the meat (usually chicken or beef). Also, fajitas don't tend to come fully wrapped like a burrito. It's more a fold-up-one-end-fold-in-the-sides-and-get-going affair.

HOW TO ROLL A BURRITO

We've never met someone who can roll a burrito perfectly on the first try. Such people don't exist. But if you give it just a tiny bit of effort, it is completely possible to avoid having your meal explode all over your lap. You just have to follow our simple steps.

First, though, there are some things you need to know to make sure you give yourself the best chance of success. It's our duty to share these with you. For a start don't buy shit tortillas. Your tortilla needs to be large enough and strong enough and have enough elasticity to do the job. On that note here's where we recommend that you go for the largest wheat flour (stronger than corn) tortillas you can find at the supermarket, with the shortest shelf life. What the hell does short shelf life mean? An expiry date of ten days max. Any longer than that and you might as well try rolling your burrito in Matzah bread.

Next, properly heat your tortillas. If they're cold they will not roll well. Warm each tortilla for about 20–30 seconds on each side, or until softened, in a dry frying pan set over a medium heat. Be careful the tortillas don't harden, blister or burn. When each one is perfect, transfer it to the side and move on to layering in the ingredients.

If you're heating up a whole batch of tortillas at once, put the warmed tortillas into a plastic container lined with paper towels. Just stack them on top of each other. Once you're done heating them all, cover with another paper towel and close the lid until you are ready to use them. The tortillas will stay warm for about 10 minutes or so.

Finally, before we get onto the actual burrito rolling, you need foil. Foil isn't just a restaurant gimmick to make our products look shiny and appealing. It's essential. Even at home. It keeps everything together. For every burrito, you'll need a square of foil that roughly matches the diameter of your tortilla. And, at the risk of getting ahead of ourselves, don't completely unwrap the burrito from its foil in order to eat it. Peel off the foil like a coil, little by little, as you go. Okay. The rolling.

LAYER Lay out your foil and place the warm tortilla on top. Then, layer in the fillings. It's super important to stripe them in nice lines, across the centre of the tortilla. This way you'll get all the flavours throughout the whole burrito. Leave a 20-percent margin or so at each end of the stripes to give you enough tortilla to parcel up.

FOLD Take the side of the burrito closest to you and fold it over the filling, all the way to the other side.

RAKE With your thumbs on the folded side of the tortilla and your fingers on the open side, rake the top half the tortilla backwards, pulling together all the ingredients within until they are nice and snug between your thumbs and fingers. Don't squeeze too hard, though. You don't want your fillings to escape (rookie mistake).

TUCK Then tuck in each end to completely encase the filling like a parcel. Try not to undo your good work with the raking by letting go completely. You'll need to pretend you have more than two hands.

ROLL Once your fillings are tucked in like your favourite baby at bedtime, you're ready to roll the parcel forwards. Keep going until you've got the loose end of the tortilla safely underneath. Then, slide that baby back to the top of the foil square.

WRAP Keeping everything nice and tight, wrap up the burrito with the foil, rolling forward (in the same direction you rolled the tortilla), taking the foil with you. Twist the ends of the foil to secure. Hey presto! The burrito is ready. (Remember: uncoil the foil *as you eat*.)

The first few times you do this your burritos will be shit. Seriously, they will pretty much suck. So if you have guests, try doing it a few times before everyone arrives and you'll get the hang of it.

LAYER

FOLD

RAKE

TUCK

ROLL

WRAP

COOKING KNOW-HOW

CHARRING

We love charred (blackened) vegetables – they give an extra smoky layer to our burritos. There are different ways to char, and the one you choose will depend on the quantity of produce you're charring and how much time you have. The aim is to blacken so that the vegetables (or fruit, garlic or chilli) are crispy with a nice char throughout.

Whichever method you choose, remember that the black flakes of charred skin or flesh are the flavour, so don't remove them. It's hard to go wrong: when in doubt leave it and char some more.

USING A FLAME A blowtorch or gas flame is probably the quickest way to char. To use a blow torch, put whatever you're charring onto a heatproof surface and turn it occasionally until the skin blackens and blisters. If using a gas flame, carefully hold the vegetable over the flame with tongs, turning it occasionally, until charred all over.

GRILLING To char large quantities of ingredients, say tomatoes, use a grill. Preheat the grill to its highest setting, put the vegetables under and turn occasionally, until charred all over.

Alternatively, use a ridged griddle pan preheated over a high heat. Place the vegetables (or whatever you're charring) in the hot pan and, as before, turn occasionally until charred all over.

TOASTING & DRY ROASTING

Toasting and dry roasting are pretty much the same. Like toasting bread, you change the flavour and texture of the food, opening up the flavour of spices and reducing the onion sharpness of garlic. To toast spices, simply pop them into a dry, heavy frying pan over a medium heat and cook until they become aromatic. Be careful not to blacken or burn the spices. Aromatic is the key word, here. To dry roast garlic, do exactly the same, leaving the cloves in their skins. Keep going until the cloves blacken and the flesh inside is soft.

KNOW YOUR CHILLIES

FRESH CHILLIES

We've tried to minimize headaches by not being too prescriptive about the fresh chillies you use in your burritos – their availability is limited at the best of times, let alone in the darkest days of November.

The following (matched up in the photograph over the page) are easily available in supermarkets across the nation. Most come in red or green versions, with red giving a more mellow flavour and green giving slightly more heat.

1 JALAPEÑO This is a shorter and fatter chilli, but hotter than its bird's eye or unnamed neighbours. We've roasted quite a few in the making of this book and they are p-e-r-f-e-c-t for adding heat without burning the house down.

2 BIRD'S EYE Also sold as Thai chillies, these fiery delights are used frequently in Asian cooking, and tend to be widely stocked in supermarkets throughout the UK. Their heat varies, as does their flavour, but we've used them predominantly to add a bit of kick on the top of various dishes.

3 HABANERO & SCOTCH BONNET These two are chilli cousins. You'll find the Scotch Bonnet a touch fruitier if eaten on its own, and we don't envy the guy who put that on Wikipedia. The citrus notes make these chillies better fresh than dried. They're the hottest chillies we've used in the recipes – try not to rub your eyes after chopping.

4 SERRANO There are some UK serrano growers out there, but the chillies will appear for sale only from July to September. The heat supercedes jalapeño and the chilli itself is far fleshier. If you can get hold of them, they're worth it; but if not use jalapeños. Keep the seeds in if you're after a little more heat than the recipe prescribes.

DRIED CHILLIES

Your new storecupboard favourites! Everyone seems to be a little scared of dried chillies in the UK, but these guys have every opportunity to be your new BFFs.

⑤ CHIPOTLES EN ADOBO This one shouldn't really be in the chilli section as it's more like a sauce-type thing. It's effectively chipotles brining in a red, sweet 'n' sticky adobo sauce. On occasion you'll see shelves stocked with chipotles en adobo puréed into one sticky paste, but mostly you'll find whole chipotles in the adobo in a jar or tin. All major supermarkets stock something of this nature – just take a look in the tin and jar section. By the way, think of the smoky–sweet chipotles en adobo as a flavour enhancer for more than just your burritos: use it to spice up a spag bol, rub it into your Sunday roast beef. YUM.

⑥ CHIPOTLE A chipotle is a smoked, dried jalapeño. Its smoky flavour adds an amazing background colour to any dish – which makes it really bloody hard to substitute. Nope. Sorry. We're afraid you're going to have to just get these guys.

⑦ GUAJILLO The guajillo is fairly sweet and mild, intended to tickle your taste buds, not blow you away. We use this one in a couple of the salsas to give them a kick. If you can't get hold of guajillo, you can substitute little by little with any other non-smoked dried chilli.

⑧ CHIPOTLE MECO Used for its powerful, deep, smoky flavour, this dried chilli basically looks like a chipotle gone wrong, or off; a bit like a leathery cigar. But, worry not! This distinctive chipotle starts out growing as a fresh jalapeño and is picked only after it starts to dry out, then it is smoked twice as long as a regular chipotle. We're sure there's a moving story about a lone farmer with an over-supply of jalapeños who had to come up with a plan for gathering together his betrothed daughter's dowry, but – sorry – we don't know it. You can substitute with some extra chipotle if you're finding the chipotle meco hard to come by.

9 CASCABEL Disguising itself as a dried cherry – *please!* – this is also known as a rattle chilli, as the seeds will come loose and make a noise inside, like a rattle. See? Relatively mild, this dried chilli is used for its earthy, nutty tones. It's great in a supporting role, but gets a bit lost as the leading lady.

10 ARBOL When dried, most chillies lose their vibrant colour – not the arbol! Our Red Taquería Salsa (see p.54) relies on the glorious arbol for colour, as well as its medium heat. You could swap it for cayenne pepper, but you'll lose some vibrant magnificence.

11 ANCHO This is a dried poblano chilli by a different name, and from Puebla, a state in east-central Mexico. *Ancho* means wide – you guessed it: it's quite large and, well, wide, and also dry-smoked. Its "green" flavour and mild fieriness are best compared to the difference between the red and green paprikas you'd buy in the supermarket. Our Puebla Chicken Mole (see p.80) is laced with a handful of these guys and in Mexico they'll be stuffed with all sorts and eaten whole.

12 PASILLA The name for a dried chilaca pepper, the pasilla (sometimes translated as "little raisin") is longer and thinner than an ancho chilli, but not too dissimilar in flavour and usefulness. It provides the sweetness in the Holy Trinity of chilli flavourings (sweetness, heat and smokiness), and also has earthy tones. Originally cultivated as a green chilli, it becomes the pasilla once the green turns to brown. If it's dried even longer, it becomes a "chilli negro".

PART TWO

THE EXTRAS

RICE & BEANS

WHEN IT COMES TO MAKING A BURRITO, RICE (AND, OKAY, SOMETIMES QUINOA) AND BEANS ARE LIKE THE MORTAR OF A BUILDING – THEY ARE THE ESSENTIAL GLUE THAT HOLDS EVERYTHING TOGETHER, PROVIDING THE SUPPORT THAT MAKES THE BUILDING STAND PROUD. BUT, TRUTH IS, NO BUILDER WOULD CONSTRUCT A BUILDING USING ONLY THE MORTAR (HOW VERY HIP IF THEY DID). SIMILARLY, YOU'RE UNLIKELY TO MAKE A BURRITO USING ONLY THE RICE AND BEANS. SO JOIN US IN PAYING HOMAGE TO THE RECIPES IN THIS SECTION WITHOUT GIVING THEM ANY IDEAS ABOVE THEIR STATION. EVERYTHING IN ITS PLACE.

SPICY CHILLI RICE

We've tried countless times to introduce spicy chilli rice into our restaurants – there is, however, some nervousness about it. It's one of our finest concoctions, so, not to be defeated, we're giving it to you in the book. All we can say is: don't worry. It will elevate the other fillings in your burrito, not burn your house down.

YOU WILL NEED

15g chipotle meco chillies

250g tomatoes, charred (see p.26)

1 large garlic clove, dry roasted (see p.26)

1 handful of coriander, leaves and stalks separated, leaves chopped

juice of 1½ limes

1 teaspoon sea salt

15g achiote paste

1 teaspoon ground cumin

300g basmati rice, washed

2 spring onions, charred (see p.26) and roughly chopped

1½ teaspoons vegetable oil

Place the chipotle mecos in a heatproof bowl and cover with just-boiled water. Press the chillies down to submerge, then leave to soak for 20 minutes, until softened. Drain, reserving 350ml of the soaking water, then remove the stems but not the seeds. Roughly chop the chillies.

Put 100g of the tomatoes in a blender with the garlic, coriander stalks, rehydrated chillies, three-quarters of the lime juice, and the salt, achiote paste, cumin and reserved cooking water and blend until smooth.

Roughly chop the remaining tomatoes and put them in a saucepan over a medium heat. Add the rice, spring onions and blended tomato mixture, then stir well. Bring up to the boil, then turn the heat down to its lowest setting, cover the pan with a tight-fitting lid and cook for 15–20 minutes, until the rice is tender and the sauce has been absorbed. Turn off the heat, and leave the rice to rest for 5 minutes on the warm hob, then add the coriander leaves, the remaining lime juice and the oil. Turn with a fork until combined. Fluff up the rice before serving.

CORIANDER & LIME RICE

This is Chilango's rice! It's universal, it's fresh, and its acidity cuts through a burrito's other flavours nicely. We've been quite prescriptive with the rice and lime juice, but please do taste before you serve – it's what our guys 'n' gals in the restaurants do, as rice will behave according to circumstance.

YOU WILL NEED

250g basmati rice, washed

1 teaspoon sea salt

1 bunch of coriander, leaves and stalks finely chopped

2 tablespoons lime juice

Put the rice in a heavy-based saucepan with 455ml of water and the salt. Place over a high heat and bring up to the boil. Cover with a tight-fitting lid, reduce the heat to its lowest setting and simmer for 15–20 minutes, until the rice is tender. Turn off the heat, and leave the rice to rest for 5 minutes on the warm hob. Fluff up the rice with a fork.

Tip the rice into a large bowl, add the remaining ingredients and stir thoroughly. Serve straightaway before the coriander turns limp, but if cooking in advance, add the coriander at the last minute.

ARROZ MEXICANA

This is our version of *arroz rojo* – a red rice, widely used in Mexican cuisine. We make ours with charred cherry tomatoes and hot chilli powder to give some backbone heat.

YOU WILL NEED

60g unsalted butter

1 small white onion, finely chopped

2 large garlic cloves, crushed

225g cherry tomatoes, charred (see p.26)

½ teaspoon dried oregano, preferably Mexican

1 teaspoon sea salt

1 tablespoon medium chilli powder

250g basmati rice, washed

Melt half the butter in a heavy-based saucepan over a medium heat. Add the onion, garlic and 2 tablespoons of water and stir until combined. Reduce the heat to low and cook gently for 10 minutes, stirring occasionally, until the onion and garlic are softened, but not browned.

Put the onion mixture in a blender. Add 250ml of water and the cherry tomatoes, oregano, salt and chilli powder and blend until smooth.

Melt the remaining butter in the saucepan over a medium–low heat. Add the rice and stir for 2 minutes to coat, then stir in the chilli-tomato purée. Bring up to the boil, then turn the heat down to its lowest setting, cover the pan with a tight-fitting lid and cook for 15–20 minutes, until the rice is tender. Turn off the heat, and leave the rice to rest for 5 minutes on the warm hob. Fluff up the rice with a fork before serving.

CLOCKWISE FROM TOP: **SPICY CHILLI RICE (P.36), CORIANDER & LIME RICE (P.37), ARROZ MEXICANA (P.37), ARROZ VERDE (P.40), CARAMELIZED COCONUT RICE (P.41)**

ARROZ VERDE

Green rice! It's green because you'll be blending in chillies, cos lettuce leaves and herbs – which sounds odder than it tastes. You'll find this included in quite a few of the burrito recipes, and frankly we think it's a winner.

YOU WILL NEED

60g unsalted butter

1 small white onion, diced

2 large garlic cloves, crushed

250g basmati rice, washed

FOR THE GREEN SAUCE

100g green chillies, such as bird's eye, deseeded and stems removed

30g green jalapeño chillies, deseeded and stems removed

12 large basil leaves

1 bunch of coriander

generous ½ bunch of flat-leaf parsley

2 spring onions, roughly chopped

30g cos lettuce leaves, or other crisp green lettuce leaves

1 teaspoon sea salt

First, make the green sauce. Put all the sauce ingredients in a blender with 240ml of water and blend to a purée – it should make about 600ml, so top up with extra water, if needed. Set aside.

Melt half the butter in a heavy-based saucepan over a medium heat. Add the onion, garlic and 2 tablespoons of water and stir until combined. Reduce the heat to low and cook gently for 10 minutes, stirring occasionally, until softened, but not browned.

Add the rice to the pan with the remaining butter and stir for 2 minutes to coat. Stir in the green sauce. Bring up to the boil, then turn the heat down to its lowest setting, cover the pan with a tight-fitting lid and cook for 15–20 minutes, until the rice is tender and the sauce has been absorbed. Turn off the heat and leave the rice to rest for 5 minutes on the warm hob. Fluff up the rice with a fork before serving.

CARAMELIZED COCONUT RICE

SERVES 4–6

Variety is the spice of life, as they say. This coconut rice is to go with some of the Asian-inspired burritos in the book – although the coconut cream makes this rice a delicious accompaniment to pretty much any food in your life.

YOU WILL NEED

300g jasmine rice, washed

1 teaspoon sea salt

300g coconut cream

30g palm sugar or light brown soft sugar

Put the rice, salt and 455ml of water in a saucepan, stir, place over a high heat and bring to the boil. Cover with a tight-fitting lid, turn the heat down to its lowest setting and cook for about 15–20 minutes, until the rice is tender and the water has been absorbed. Turn off the heat and leave the rice to rest for 5 minutes on the warm hob.

While the rice is cooking, put the coconut cream and sugar in a small saucepan and place over a high heat. Bring to the boil and allow to continue boiling for 1 minute. Set aside.

Once the rice has rested, pour over the sweetened coconut mixture, folding it in gently until completely combined. Remove the pan from the hob and serve immediately.

HOT MEXICAN QUINOA

Yeah, yeah. Normally you'd put rice in a burrito, but the world is a diverse place, so we can definitely mix things up a little. Here (and over there), quinoa is a burrito filler. This version is served hot, straight from the hob, making it a worthy alternative to a rice option. Made with smoky chipotle, this is not your standard shop-bought lunch salad, but actually something you'd come back for.

YOU WILL NEED

1 dried chipotle meco chilli

2 teaspoons vegetable oil

5 green jalapeño chillies, charred (see p.26) and thinly sliced

2 garlic cloves, crushed

250g quinoa

1 teaspoon smoked paprika

4 tablespoons orange juice

1 tablespoon lime juice

1 litre vegetable stock

1 teaspoon sea salt

2 spring onions, charred (see p.26) and sliced

2 tomatoes, charred (see p.26) and chopped

1 corn on the cob, charred (see p.26) and kernels removed

125g tinned black beans, drained and rinsed

1 handful of chopped coriander leaves

Place the meco chilli in a heatproof bowl and cover with just-boiled water. Press the chilli down to submerge, then leave to soak for 20 minutes, until softened. Drain and remove the stem, leaving the seeds, and finely chop.

To cook the quinoa using the risotto method, heat the oil in a saucepan over a medium heat, add the meco and jalapeño chillies and the garlic and cook for 2 minutes, stirring. Add the quinoa and stir until coated in the chilli mixture.

Next, add the smoked paprika, and the orange and lime juices, and a third of the stock. Cook, stirring, until the liquid has been absorbed. Pour in another third of the stock and cook, stirring, until the liquid has been absorbed again, and then repeat with the last of the stock, and until the quinoa is soft, but still has a slight bite.

Taste for seasoning, adding salt if you feel it needs it, turn off the heat and leave the quinoa to rest for 5 minutes, covered. Fluff up with a fork and then spoon the quinoa into a serving bowl. Fold in the remaining ingredients before serving.

MANGO & AVO QUINOA

We know – two recipes where we provide quinoa as a substitute for rice. Don't worry, we won't push our luck any further. This is a cold, fruity, Mexican-inspired quinoa to fill your burritos.

YOU WILL NEED

200g quinoa

1 tomato, charred (see p.26), deseeded and chopped

2 shallots, charred (see p.26), chopped

1 green jalapeño chilli, charred (see p.26) and thinly sliced

1 large corn on the cob, charred (see p.26) and kernels removed

100g tinned pinto beans

1 small ripe mango, charred (see p.26), stone and skin removed, flesh cubed

1 small ripe Hass avocado, halved, stoned, and flesh cut into small pieces

1 small bunch of coriander, leaves and stalks finely chopped

juice of 1 lime

1 teaspoon sea salt

Cook the quinoa following the packet instructions, then drain if necessary. Transfer to a serving bowl, fluff up with a fork and leave to cool.

Add the tomato, shallots, jalapeño, corn kernels, beans, mango, avocado, coriander and lime juice. Season with the salt and toss until combined. Best eaten straightaway, or within a few hours at most.

THIS PAGE (TOP TO BOTTOM): **HOT MEXICAN QUINOA (P.42), MANGO & AVO QUINOA (P.43)**
OPPOSITE (TOP TO BOTTOM): **CHARRO BEANS (P.46), CHIPOTLE BLACK BEANS (P.47)**

CHARRO BEANS

Charro beans are eaten in the very north of Mexico close to the US border (as a general rule of thumb, you eat pinto beans north of Mexico City and black beans south of it). Cross the border into the US (with or without wall – at the time of writing, we don't know) and these are "cowboy beans", usually served with some shredded bacon or minced beef. This recipe includes bacon, but you can leave it out for a vegetarian version.

YOU WILL NEED

250g dried pinto beans, soaked overnight, then drained and rinsed (or use tinned; see note, below)

1 white onion, finely chopped

2 garlic cloves, chopped

60g smoked bacon lardons (optional)

1 green jalapeño chilli, sliced

1 tablespoon sliced chipotles en adobo

225g tomatoes, charred (see p.26), deseeded and finely chopped

1 teaspoon dried oregano, preferably Mexican

½ teaspoon sea salt, plus extra to taste (optional)

Put the beans into a large saucepan, then cover with 1.2 litres of cold water. Place over a high heat and bring to the boil. Boil for 10 minutes, skimming off any scum as it rises. Add the onion and garlic, then turn the heat down to low and simmer, covered, for 1½–2 hours, or until tender and creamy. Check the water during cooking and top up if necessary.

Ten minutes before the beans are ready, heat a large sauté pan over a medium heat. Add the bacon, if using, and cook for 5 minutes without turning, until the fat starts to run. Add the chilli, chipotles en adobo, tomatoes, oregano and 100ml of water and cook for 5 minutes, stirring occasionally.

Check to see if the beans are ready and most of the water has evaporated. If there is still a lot of water in the pan, drain the beans slightly – they should be a little wet, rather than completely dry. Add the sautéed tomato mixture and the salt to the beans and cook for another 15 minutes over a low heat, stirring occasionally, until thoroughly heated through. Taste, adding extra salt, if needed.

USING TINNED PINTO BEANS

To use tinned pinto beans instead of dried beans, drain and rinse 2½ x 400g cans pinto beans. Fry the onion in 1 tablespoon vegetable oil over a medium heat for 8 minutes, then add the garlic and cook for another minute. Blend the onion mixture in a mini food processor or blender with the chilli and tomato mixture (see method, above). Cook the tinned beans with the tomato mixture in a saucepan for 10 minutes, until heated through. Taste, adding extra salt, if needed.

SERVES 4-6

CHIPOTLE BLACK BEANS

Black beans have been filling burritos since time immemorial. Using dried beans delivers a better end result, but – we hear ya – it is quite a lot of prep. Feel free to use drained tinned black beans instead (see the handy note below). The chipotle en adobo goes a long way to achieving flavour – it's easily available online.

YOU WILL NEED

350g dried black beans, soaked overnight, then drained and rinsed (or use tinned; see note, below)

1 small white onion, finely chopped

6 garlic cloves, finely chopped

3 bay leaves

1 dried pasilla chilli

½ tablespoon olive oil

2 teaspoons ground cumin

60g chipotles en adobo

250g tomatoes, charred (see p.26), deseeded and roughly chopped

1 rounded tablespoon tomato purée

1 teaspoon sea salt, plus extra to taste (optional)

juice of ½ lime (optional)

Tip the soaked beans into a large saucepan, then cover with 1.5 litres of water. Place over a high heat and bring to the boil. Boil for 10 minutes, skimming off any scum as it rises. Add the onion, garlic and bay, then turn the heat down to low and simmer, covered, for 1½–2 hours, or until tender and creamy. Check the water during cooking and top up if necessary.

While the beans are cooking, place the pasilla chilli in a heatproof bowl and cover with just-boiled water. Press the chilli down to submerge, then leave to soak for 20 minutes, until softened. Drain the chilli, then remove the stem and seeds and roughly chop. Discard the soaking water. Transfer to a mini food processor or blender with the oil, cumin, chipotles en adobo, tomatoes, tomato purée and salt and blend to a purée.

Check to see if the beans are ready and most of the water has evaporated. If there is still a lot of water in the pan, drain the beans slightly – they should be just a little wet. Remove the bay leaves and add the blended tomato mixture. Stir and heat through for 5 minutes. Taste, adding lime juice and extra salt, if needed.

TO MAKE REFRIED BEANS

Heat 1 tablespoon of olive oil in a large frying pan over a medium heat, add 1 recipe quantity of chipotle black beans, and fry, stirring and mashing the beans using a potato masher or the back of a fork, for 5 minutes, or until soft and broken down. Remove from the heat, and season, if necessary.

USING TINNED BLACK BEANS

To use tinned black beans instead of dried beans, drain and rinse 2½ x 400g cans black beans. Fry the onion in 1 tablespoon vegetable oil over a medium heat for 8 minutes, then add the garlic and cook for another minute. Blend the onion mixture in a mini food processor or blender with the pasilla chilli and tomato mixture (see method, above). Cook the tinned beans with the tomato mixture in a saucepan for 10 minutes, until heated through. Taste, adding extra salt, if needed.

SALSAS, GUACS & CREMAS

SALSAS, GUACAMOLES AND CREMAS (INSIDE, ON THE SIDE, OR IN SLAW) ARE A HALLMARK OF MEXICAN COOKING. IN FACT, WE'D BE LOST WITHOUT THEM. TO OMIT THEM IS SORT OF LIKE HAVING YOUR SUNDAY ROAST WITHOUT GRAVY. ALL THE RECIPES IN THIS SECTION HAVE BEEN DEVELOPED WITH SUPERMARKET SHOPPING IN MIND. AND (MORE CHILANGO WORDS OF WISDOM), WHEN IT COMES TO TOMATOES, PLEASE DO USE THOSE SPECIFIED IN THE INGREDIENTS AND REMEMBER IT'S WORTH SPENDING THOSE EXTRA PENNIES ON THE BEST YOU CAN BUY – NOT ALL TOMATOES ARE CREATED EQUAL AND FLAVOUR IS EVERYTHING.

SMOKY CORN SALSA

SERVES 4

Corn is the potato of Mexico. A pointless comment, but it's true.

YOU WILL NEED

4 corn on the cobs, kernels stripped
    (you'll need about 400g of kernels)
2 tablespoons Pickled Onions (see
    below) with a little of the pickling
    liquid
100g green bird's eye chillies, charred
    (see p.26), deseeded and diced
100g red bird's eye chillies, charred
    (see p.26), deseeded and diced
sea salt

FOR THE PICKLED ONIONS

1 large red onion, thinly sliced
50–75ml cider vinegar
½ teaspoon sea salt

First, you'll need to make the pickled onions. Bring a small saucepan of water to the boil and add the onion slices. Boil for 1 minute, to soften, then drain and rinse under cold water. Pour 50ml of the cider vinegar into a small bowl with 50ml of water. Add the salt, then the drained onion slices. Stir to combine and transfer to a lidded jar. The liquid should cover the onion – if it doesn't, top up with equal amounts of extra vinegar and water. Seal the jar and store in the fridge for up to 2 weeks.

To make the salsa, first, dry roast the corn. Heat a large, non-stick frying pan over a high heat until very hot. Add half the corn and toast for 3–5 minutes, without stirring, until the kernels start to pop, blacken and caramelize. Stir once and continue to dry roast, without stirring, for another 3 minutes. Colour is most important here, you want the kernels to char, but still be crisp. Tip the kernels into a serving bowl and repeat to dry roast the remaining half.

Add the pickled onions to the corn and stir in the green and red chillies. Season with salt to taste.

ROASTED PINEAPPLE SALSA

SERVES 4

We love, love, LOVE this salsa. Some spice and tropical zing, with amazing char notes. During the tastings for this book, we probably put it on half the dishes.

YOU WILL NEED

1 ripe pineapple, peeled and cut into
    1cm-thick rings
1 green habanero chilli
1 red bird's eye chilli
juice of 1 lime
1 teaspoon caster sugar
1 handful of chopped coriander leaves

Place the pineapple in a large, dry frying pan over a medium–low heat, and gently caramelize for about 4–5 minutes on each side, until light golden in places. Make sure that it doesn't darken too much, otherwise it will taste burnt. Remove from the pan and cut the pineapple into small dice, discarding the core from each ring. Wipe the pan clean and dry roast both types of chilli over a low heat for about 10 minutes, until they begin to blacken. Remove the stems and seeds.

To assemble the salsa, put the pineapple in a mixing bowl and stir in the rest of the ingredients.

ROASTED HABANERO SALSA

SERVES 4-6

Habaneros have an amazing, fruity flavour beneath all the heat. And, trust me, there is heat in this salsa. Whatever you do, don't rub your eyes – or scratch anywhere downstairs – after handling a habanero.

YOU WILL NEED

500g tomatoes

1 onion, cut into wedges

1 red pepper, deseeded and quartered

1 red habanero chilli

2 large garlic cloves, dry roasted
   (see p.26)

1 tablespoon olive oil

juice of 1 lime

1 teaspoon sea salt, plus extra to taste
   (optional)

1 handful of chopped coriander leaves

Preheat the oven to 180°C/350°F/Gas 4. Put the tomatoes, onion, red pepper, chilli and garlic in a large roasting tin, then drizzle over the oil and turn until coated. Roast for 15–20 minutes, removing the chilli after 5 minutes. The vegetables and garlic should be softened, but still retain a bit of crunch. Remove the seeds from the chilli, if you prefer a milder-tasting salsa.

Put the roasted ingredients in a food processor and pulse briefly to make a chunky salsa. CHUNKY! Tip the salsa into a bowl and stir in the lime juice, salt and coriander. Taste and add more salt, if you think it needs it.

SMOKY TOMATO SALSA

SERVES 6

Good with steaks and smoky meats. Done.

YOU WILL NEED

1 tablespoon olive oil

350g white onions, finely chopped

2 large garlic cloves, dry roasted
   (see p.26)

25g chipotles en adobo

500g small tomatoes, charred
   (see p.26)

½ teaspoon smoked salt, preferably
   mesquite

½ teaspoon sea salt

1 teaspoon red wine vinegar

1 teaspoon chipotle powder

Heat the oil in a large sauté pan over a medium–low heat, add the onions and cook gently, stirring often, for 15–20 minutes, until softened and starting to colour. Turn the heat down to low if they start to burn.

Put the onion, garlic and chipotles en adobo in a food processor, or use a hand blender, and process to a coarse purée. Add the rest of the ingredients and pulse again briefly – do not over blend; you want the salsa to be slightly chunky.

THIS PAGE (CLOCKWISE FROM TOP): **SMOKY CORN SALSA (P.50)**, **ROASTED PINEAPPLE SALSA (P.50)**, **ROASTED HABANERO SALSA (P.51)** CENTRE (BOTTOM) **SMOKY TOMATO SALSA (P.51)** OPPOSITE (CLOCKWISE FROM TOP): **TOMATILLO & AVOCADO SALSA (P.54)**, **RED TAQUERÍA SALSA (P.54)**, **PICO DE GALLO (P.55)**, **SALSA VERDE (P.55)**

TOMATILLO & AVOCADO SALSA

YOU WILL NEED

500g tinned tomatillos, drained well

½ small white onion, roughly chopped

2 green jalapeño chillies, roughly chopped

1 handful of coriander leaves

¾ teaspoon sea salt

¾ teaspoon caster sugar

1 teaspoon lime juice

1 ripe Hass avocado, halved, stoned and flesh scooped out

The creaminess of the mashed avocado takes the edge off the sharpness of the tomatillos. I remember practically drinking this one in Mexico City, when I rocked up to a taco stand after a long night out.

Put the tomatillos, onion, jalapeños and coriander in a blender and blend to a coarse purée. Add the salt, sugar, lime juice and avocado and pulse briefly to make a coarse salsa. Do not over blend – we wanna see avocado lumps.

RED TAQUERÍA SALSA

As standard to a taquería as vinegar is to a chippy, this is a runny salsa that will make any steak at least three times more interesting. You can also bottle it up and store it in the fridge for a rainy day.

YOU WILL NEED

8 dried arbol chillies

2 dried guajillo chillies

1 dried cascabel chilli

300g tomatoes, charred (see p.26)

3 garlic cloves, dry roasted (see p.26)

20g caster sugar

2 tablespoons white wine vinegar

¾ teaspoon sea salt

Place all the dried chillies in a heatproof bowl and cover with just-boiled water. Press the chillies down to submerge, then leave to soak for 20 minutes, until softened. Drain, reserving the soaking water, and remove the stems and seeds. Roughly chop the chillies.

Put the chillies in a blender with the rest of the ingredients and 100ml of the soaking water, then blitz until smooth. Pour into a saucepan and cook over a low heat for 10 minutes, stirring occasionally, until reduced slightly. The sauce should be runny like soy sauce, so add more of the soaking water, if you need to.

PICO DE GALLO

SERVES 4–6

Pico de Gallo, sometimes called *salsa fresca*, is Mexico's most common salsa – you'll find it at taquerías, in restaurants... with chips. The name means "prick (or beak) of the rooster", so make sure it has peck... no dumbing down. Made fresh, it's a far cry from jarred supermarket versions. It's the raw, bright counterpoint to the cooked foods, which is such an important flavour dynamic in Mexican cuisine.

YOU WILL NEED

500g very ripe plum tomatoes, deseeded and diced

¼ teaspoon sea salt

1 red onion, diced

10g roughly chopped coriander leaves

½ small serrano chilli or hot green or red bird's eye chilli, finely diced

juice of ½ lime

1½ teaspoons lemon juice

1½ tablespoons olive oil

Put the tomatoes in a colander and sprinkle over the salt, then turn until combined. Suspend the colander over a bowl and leave to drain for 10 minutes. Discard any tomato juices in the bowl.

Tip the tomatoes into a serving bowl, stir in the rest of the ingredients and gently turn until combined. Serve within a few hours of making.

SALSA VERDE

SERVES 4–6

This is the spiciest salsa we offer at Chilango and it goes especially well with beef. It's best made with fresh tomatillos, but tinned make an easy substitute.

YOU WILL NEED

500g small fresh tomatillos, husks removed; or 500g tinned tomatillos, drained well

50g white onion, sliced

3 green jalapeño chillies

1 large handful of coriander leaves

1 teaspoon sea salt

1 teaspoon caster sugar

1 teaspoon lime juice, plus extra to taste (optional)

If using fresh tomatillos, cook them in plenty of boiling water for about 5 minutes, until softened. Plunge them into an ice bath to cool and keep their green colour, then drain well.

Cook the onion and jalapeños in boiling water for 3–4 minutes, until softened. Plunge them into an ice bath to cool, then drain well.

Put the tomatillos, onion, jalapeño and coriander in a blender, then blend briefly so the salsa is still quite chunky. Spoon into a serving bowl and stir in the salt, sugar and lime juice. Taste and add more lime juice, if needed.

SERVES
4

CLASSIC GUACAMOLE

Guacamole! Where do we start? Put a bowl of this in front of one of us and we'll eat the whole damn thing in a few minutes. This recipe is closely based on how we make our stand-out guac in the restaurants. We actually handmash our guac at least twice a day, not just because it gets gobbled up so quickly, but also because the avocados oxidize quickly once cut open. Whatever you do, DO NOT use a blender to mix your guac. It absolutely must be handmashed to have the right texture. It's a workout you'll get nowhere else (our best guac-makers do look a little like Turkish hamam masseurs). And if you buy pre-made guac in a plastic tub from the supermarket, sorry but you're no friend of ours. Let's be friends.

YOU WILL NEED

2 ripe Hass avocados, halved and stoned

½ red onion, diced

1 handful of finely chopped coriander leaves

juice of 1 lime

sea salt and ground black pepper

Scoop the avocado flesh into a bowl and mash with the back of a fork to a creamy consistency, making sure there are still chunks of avocado.

Mix in the remaining ingredients and season with salt and pepper to taste.

SERVES
4

CHARRED JALAPEÑO GUACAMOLE

All the goodness of our Chilango guacamole with some charred jalapeños.

YOU WILL NEED

2 ripe Hass avocados, halved and stoned

1 green jalapeño chilli, charred (see p.26) and finely chopped (deseed optional)

¼ red onion, diced

juice of 1 lime

sea salt and ground black pepper

Scoop the avocado flesh into a bowl and mash with the back of a fork to a creamy consistency, making sure there are still chunks of avocado.

Mix in the remaining ingredients and season with salt and pepper to taste.

TOP: **CLASSIC GUACAMOLE**
BOTTOM: **CHARRED JALAPEÑO GUACAMOLE**

CHIPOTLE CREMA

SERVES 4-6

Get this Chipotle Crema going instead of shop-bought ketchup and live a tastier life. It is mind-blowingly delicious either as an addition to the slaw on page 64, or with cheese on toast, sausages and mash, or wherever else you tend to squirt your ketchup. Adios Heinz.

YOU WILL NEED

250g thick soured cream or crème fraîche

60g chipotles en adobo, chopped

60g mayonnaise

2 teaspoons lime juice

Whisk all the ingredients together in a serving bowl until combined – we're looking for the consistency of ketchup, so add a splash of water if needed.

LIME & JALAPEÑO CREMA

SERVES 4-6

If you want to add some heat to your burrito or slaw without blowing the house down, this blackened jalapeño has gotta be your choice.

YOU WILL NEED

250g thick soured cream or crème fraîche

50g green jalapeño chillies, charred (see p.26)

1 tablespoon lime juice

1 large handful of coriander leaves

1 teaspoon sea salt

Put all the ingredients in a blender or food processor and blend until smooth. Add a splash of water to loosen, if needed.

CREMA DE COMAL

SERVES 4-6

A *comal* is a pan used in Mexico to char and toast spices, herbs and chillies (don't worry – we've suggested you use a blow torch, grill or griddle to do the job; see p.26). This crema is so-called because it plays glorious host to charred tomatillos, onion and jalapeños.

YOU WILL NEED

250g thick soured cream or crème fraîche

100g fresh tomatillos, charred (see p.26); or 100g tinned tomatillos, drained well

4 spring onions, charred (see p.26)

3–4 green jalapeño chillies, charred (see p.26) and deseeded

flesh of ½ ripe Hass avocado

¾ teaspoon liquid smoke

1 teaspoon sea salt

4 teaspoons lime juice

1 handful of coriander leaves

Put all the ingredients in a blender or food processor and blend until smooth.

ROASTED GARLIC CREMA

SERVES 4-6

We love roasting. Onions. Tomatoes. Chillies. And, of course, garlic. Roasting the garlic in this recipe elevates this crema to the Promised Land.

YOU WILL NEED

3 garlic cloves, dry roasted (see p.26)

a large pinch of ground cumin

½ teaspoon sea salt

20g mayonnaise

1 tablespoon lime juice

250g thick soured cream or crème fraîche

Put all the ingredients in a blender or food processor and blend until smooth. Add a splash of water to loosen, if needed.

CLOCKWISE FROM TOP LEFT: **CHIPOTLE CREMA (P.58)**,
**CREMA DE COMAL (P.59), LIME & JALAPEÑO CREMA
(P.58), ROASTED GARLIC CREMA (P.59)**

SLAWS & SALADS

"IT'S THE NEW MILLENNIUM SO WE'VE GOTTA INCLUDE SOMETHING WITH QUINOA." THAT'S THE EXACT BRIEF OUR FOOD-DEVELOPMENT TEAM GOT WAY BACK WHEN. TURNS OUT THIS QUINOA STUFF IS PRETTY DAMN GOOD, AND PROBABLY WHY THE SOUTH AMERICANS HAVE BEEN EATING IT FOR THE PAST 4,000 YEARS. ALONGSIDE QUINOA SALADS, IN THIS SECTION YOU'LL FIND AN ARRAY OF OTHER SALADS AND SLAWS THAT'LL BE EITHER BRILLIANT INSIDE YOUR BURRITO OR BETTER STILL SERVED UP ON THE SIDE.

BAJA CABBAGE SLAW

This is a 4-for-1 sort of deal. This slaw is great just as it is, but if you fancy something a bit creamier, mix it with one of the cremas on pages 58–9 for kicks 'n' creaminess.

YOU WILL NEED

200g white cabbage, tough stalk
    removed and leaves finely shredded
½ teaspoon sea salt
1 carrot, coarsely grated
3 spring onions, thinly sliced
1 large green bird's eye chilli,
    deseeded and finely chopped
1 handful of chopped coriander leaves
1 teaspoon lime juice
1½ tablespoons mayonnaise

Mix together all the ingredients in a serving bowl. Serve straightaway, or keep covered for a few hours in the fridge, then serve.

ROASTED PINEAPPLE SLAW IN TACO BOWLS

SERVES 4

Blackened peppers, onions, pineapple and jalapeños, together with sliced red and white cabbage, and a charred pineapple, cumin and chilli salsa will turn any idea you think you have about slaw completely on its head. Welcome to the converted.

YOU WILL NEED

½ small red cabbage, shredded

½ small white cabbage, shredded

2 carrots, grated

1 small red pepper, charred (see p.26), deseeded and diced

1 small yellow pepper, charred (see p.26), deseeded and diced

1 small red onion, sliced, charred (see p.26) and diced

50g pineapple, cored and diced

1 green jalapeño chilli, charred (see p.26)

1 handful of coriander leaves, chopped

½ teaspoon sea salt

1 teaspoon lime juice

FOR THE TACO BOWLS

vegetable oil, for brushing

4 tortillas, each about 20cm in diameter

FOR THE FRUITY DRESSING

100g pineapple, sliced into 1cm-thick slices, then charred (see p.26) and chopped

2 tablespoons orange juice

1 tablespoon lime juice

½ red bird's eye chilli, deseeded

1 teaspoon salt

¼ teaspoon cumin seeds, toasted (see p.26)

¼ teaspoon ground black pepper

First, make the taco bowls. Preheat the oven to 180°C/350°F/Gas 4. Warm the tortillas to make them more pliable, then lightly brush both sides of each with oil. Turn a deep 12-cup muffin tray upside down and nestle a tortilla between four of the cups, gathering up the sides to make a bowl shape. Repeat to make 4 bowls in total. (Alternatively, drape the warm tortillas over 4 heatproof, greased upside-down cereal bowls.) Bake for about 12–14 minutes, then remove from the tray (or bowls), place on a baking tray and bake for another 1 minute, until crisp and golden. Set aside to cool.

Make the fruity dressing. Put all the dressing ingredients in a blender and blend until smooth. Set aside.

Mix together all the slaw ingredients in a bowl until combined.

To assemble, divide the slaw between the four taco bowls and spoon the dressing over. Serve straightaway – they won't wait and you don't want the taco bowls to go soggy.

THIS PAGE: **ROASTED PINEAPPLE SLAW IN TACO BOWLS (P.65)** OPPOSITE (TOP): **CORN & BEAN SALAD (P.68)** OPPOSITE (BOTTOM): **AVOCADO & CHARRED VEG SALAD (P.69)**

SERVES
4

CORN & BEAN SALAD

This salad is probably best served when you're making tacos as it makes rather a hearty side, or even a meal in its own right. This and the Chimichurri Steak on page 107 will see you through until morning.

YOU WILL NEED

2 corn on the cobs, charred (see p.26) and kernels stripped

1 small red pepper, charred (see p.26), deseeded and diced

1 small yellow pepper, charred (see p.26), deseeded and diced

1 small red onion, charred (see p.26) and diced

100g fresh tomatillos, diced; or 100g tinned tomatillos drained well and diced

400g tin of black beans, drained and rinsed

1 teaspoon smoked paprika

½ teaspoon achiote paste

½ teaspoon cumin seeds, toasted (see p.26)

1 tablespoon vegetable oil

1 teaspoon sherry vinegar

1½ teaspoons chipotles en adobo, finely chopped

1 teaspoon agave syrup or nectar

1 teaspoon sea salt

¼ teaspoon ground black pepper

1 handful of chopped coriander leaves

Put all the vegetables and beans in a serving bowl.

Heat a large, dry frying pan over a medium–low heat. Add the paprika, achiote paste and cumin and dry roast, breaking up the achiote with the back of a spatula, for 1 minute, or until everything smells aromatic. Remove from the heat. Put the oil in a bowl and stir in the dry-roasted spice mixture.

Add the vinegar, chipotles en adobo, agave, salt and pepper to the spice oil and mix together until combined and the achiote dissolves. Pour the dressing over the vegetables, turn until combined, then scatter the coriander over the top before serving.

AVOCADO & CHARRED VEG SALAD

Just as the name says: avocado and charred veg, turned into a salad and then dressed with the Crema de Comal on page 59. Happy days.

YOU WILL NEED

2 tomatoes, charred (see p.26), roughly chopped

1 cucumber, deseeded and roughly chopped

1 corn on the cob, charred (see p.26) and kernels stripped

1 large ripe Hass avocado, halved, stoned and flesh diced

1 red onion, charred (see p.26) and diced

juice of ½ lime

½ teaspoon sea salt

1 red bird's eye chilli, deseeded and thinly sliced

1 teaspoon chipotle chilli sauce or sauce from a jar of chipotles en adobo

1 handful of chopped coriander leaves

½ recipe quantity of Crema de Comal (see p.59)

Put all the prepared vegetables in a serving bowl. In a separate small bowl, mix together the lime juice, salt, chilli, and chipotle chilli sauce. Spoon the dressing over the salad and toss gently until combined. Scatter over the coriander leaves.

A drizzle of Crema de Comal over the top of the salad adds the finishing touch. Serve any leftover crema by the side.

LONDON'S BEST BURRITOS

PART THREE

THE BURRITOS (& FRIENDS)

CHICKEN

EVERYONE LOVES TO EAT CHICKEN. WELL, EVERYONE, THAT IS, EXCEPT VEGETARIANS, PRESUMABLY. BUT EVERYONE ELSE LOVES CHICKEN. WE SERVE SO MUCH CHICKEN AT OUR RESTAURANTS THAT SOMETIMES WE SAY WE ARE A CHICKEN SHOP DRESSED IN MEXICAN CLOTHING. THE BURRITOS AND FAJITAS IN THIS CHAPTER ARE HERE TO SATISFY EVEN THE MOST FERVENT CHICKEN ENTHUSIAST. YOU'LL FIND SOME ASIAN FUSION AMONG THE MEXICANA, AND A DOUBLE-CHICKEN BURRITO INTENDED FOR DAYS WHEN YOU'RE REALLY HUNGRY (OR FEEL INCLINED TO SHARE).

CHILANGO CHICKEN

This is a simple but tasty chicken recipe, with a nice barbecue and mango tang. It's not exactly the same as the one we serve at the restaurants (we have to keep something up our sleeves), but it's close and just as tasty. Enjoy.

YOU WILL NEED

500g skinless, boneless chicken
    thighs
4 warmed tortillas

FOR THE MARINADE

1 dried ancho chilli
½ teaspoon ground black pepper
1 teaspoon sea salt
75g barbecue sauce (you could use
    the sauce from the BBQ Chipotle
    Chicken on page 91)
1 tablespoon caster sugar
½ white onion
1 red habanero chilli, roughly chopped
30g chopped mango
1½ teaspoons chipotle powder
1 teaspoon raw, unfiltered apple cider
    vinegar
1 large garlic clove, crushed
1 teaspoon dried oregano, preferably
    Mexican
1 teaspoon dried thyme

First, make the marinade. Put the ancho chilli in a small pan, cover with just-boiled water and cook for 10 minutes, until softened. Drain, discarding the soaking liquid, and remove the stem and seeds. Put the ancho with the rest of the marinade ingredients in a blender and blend to a smooth paste.

Put the chicken in a non-metallic dish, spoon the marinade over and turn until coated. Cover and leave to marinate in the fridge for 1–4 hours, or overnight if time allows – the longer, the better.

Just before you start to cook the chicken, preheat the oven to 180°C/350°F/Gas 4. Heat a large, ridged griddle pan or chargrill over a high heat until smoking hot. Add a splash of oil, then the chicken thighs, and griddle for 2 minutes, then turn the thighs 90° and cook for another 2 minutes. Turn the thighs over and repeat. Transfer the chicken to a roasting tin and cook in the oven for 10–15 minutes, or until cooked through and golden. Slice or chop the chicken, divide it into 4 equal portions and use each portion to top a warmed tortilla. Fill as below, then roll.

FILL YOUR BURRITOS

To complete your burritos, use 1 recipe quantity of:

»→ **Coriander & Lime Rice** (see p.37)
»→ **Chipotle Black Beans** (see p.47)
»→ **Pico de Gallo** (see p.55)
»→ **Smoky Tomato Salsa** (see p.51)
»→ **Chipotle Crema** (see p.58)

CHICKEN FAJITAS

I'm not a huge fan of Chicken Fajitas (I'm really selling this recipe now, right?). But what I like or dislike doesn't always matter. And this recipe is a good example, because most other people seem to love good old chicken fajitas. And that's what you get: good old chicken fajitas with the usual suspects in the spice mix, and sweetened up a little with a dash of agave.

YOU WILL NEED

500g mini skinless, boneless chicken breast fillets

2 tablespoons rapeseed oil

3 tablespoons agave syrup or nectar

1 large white onion, halved and sliced

1 large red pepper, deseeded and thinly sliced into long strips

1 large yellow pepper, deseeded and thinly sliced into long strips

1 large green pepper, deseeded and thinly sliced into long strips

1 lime, for squeezing

4 warmed tortillas

slices of charred (see p.26) green jalapeño chillies

FOR THE FAJITA SPICE MIX

2 teaspoons smoked salt, preferably mesquite

1 teaspoon ground black pepper

¾ teaspoon garlic powder

¾ teaspoon onion powder

1 teaspoon smoked paprika

2 teaspoons ground cumin

1½ teaspoons chipotle powder

½ teaspoon dried oregano, preferably Mexican

1 teaspoon chicken stock powder or crumbled chicken stock cube

In a small bowl, mix together all the ingredients for the fajita spice mix.

Put the chicken, half the oil, the agave, and 4 teaspoons of the fajita spice mix in a large mixing bowl and turn until the chicken is evenly coated.

Put the onion and peppers in another large bowl, pour over the remaining oil and remaining fajita spice mix and toss until combined.

Heat a large, ridged griddle pan or chargrill over a high heat until hot. Chargrill the seasoned vegetables in batches for about 3 minutes per batch, turning them occasionally, until they are charred in places but retain their crunch. Take care not to overload the pan – the vegetables need space, otherwise they will steam rather than chargrill. When cooked, put the vegetables in a bowl, squeeze over the juice from the lime and cover the bowl to keep the veg warm.

Wipe the griddle pan or chargrill clean with kitchen paper, then return it to a high heat. Add the spicy chicken and chargrill for 8–10 minutes, turning once, until cooked through and golden.

Divide the chicken strips into 4 equal portions and serve on top of the warmed tortillas with the vegetables and fillings (see below) and sprinkled with the sliced jalapeños.

FILL YOUR FAJITAS

To complete your burritos, use 1 recipe quantity of:

»→ **Roasted Pineapple Salsa (see p.50)**

»→ **Classic Guacamole (see p.56)**

»→ **Roasted Garlic Crema (see p.59)**

CHICKEN TINGA

I first tasted Chicken Tinga in Mexico City, although the dish originates from Puebla. A combination of tomatoes, peppers, onion, garlic and smoky chipotle, with thyme and a dash of sweetness from the balsamic vinegar and the dark brown sugar, after a long night out it really hit the spot.

YOU WILL NEED

500g skinless, boneless chicken thighs

4 warmed tortillas

coriander leaves

grated Cheddar cheese

sea salt and ground black pepper

FOR THE TINGA SAUCE

3 dried chipotle chillies

3 tablespoons olive oil

1 large white onion, thinly sliced

2 large red peppers, deseeded and thinly sliced

1 tablespoon tomato purée

450g small tomatoes, charred (see p.26)

200ml tomato juice

4 garlic cloves, charred (see p.26)

60g chipotles en adobo

½ teaspoon thyme leaves

½ teaspoon sea salt, plus extra for seasoning

¼ teaspoon ground black pepper, plus extra for seasoning

⅓ teaspoon smoked salt, preferably mesquite

1 tablespoon balsamic vinegar

2 teaspoons dark brown soft sugar

To make the tinga sauce, place the chipotle chillies in a heatproof bowl and cover with just-boiled water. Press the chillies down to submerge, then leave to soak for 20 minutes, until softened. Drain the chillies and remove the stems and seeds.

Heat 2 tablespoons of the olive oil in a large, lidded sauté pan over a low heat. Add the onion and cook gently, covered and stirring regularly, for about 20 minutes, until soft, but not coloured.

Stir in the red peppers and cook, covered, for 10 minutes more, stirring occasionally. Stir in the rest of the sauce ingredients, cover and simmer gently for 20 minutes, until reduced and thickened.

Meanwhile, season the chicken with salt and pepper. Heat the remaining oil in a large frying pan and sauté the chicken for 8–10 minutes, or until cooked through and golden. Cut the chicken into pieces.

Stir the chicken into the tinga sauce and heat through for 5 minutes before dividing into 4 equal portions, using each portion to top a warmed tortilla. Fill as below, sprinkle with coriander leaves and cheese to taste, then roll.

FILL YOUR BURRITOS

To complete your burritos, use 1 recipe quantity of:

»→ **Coriander & Lime Rice** (see p.37)

»→ **Salsa Verde** (see p.55)

»→ **Roasted Garlic Crema** (see p.59)

»→ **Pickled Onions** (see p.50)

CLOCKWISE FROM TOP LEFT: **CHICKEN FAJITAS (P.76), CHICKEN TINGA (P.77), PUEBLA CHICKEN MOLE (P.80), YUCATÁN ACHIOTE MARINATED CHICKEN (P.81)**

PUEBLA CHICKEN MOLE

Moles are the zenith of Mexican sauces – more complex and layered than any other. Use brightly coloured dried chillies that are pliable, which shows they are from a new crop, rather than those that are broken and brittle.

YOU WILL NEED

4 large dried ancho chillies

3 dried guajillo chillies

2 dried pasilla chillies

2 dried chipotle chillies

75g raisins

3 large garlic cloves, dry roasted (see p.26)

1 small white onion, sliced into rings and charred (see p.26)

450g tomatoes, charred (see p.26)

85g toasted flaked almonds

1 teaspoon ground cinnamon

½ teaspoon ground allspice

a large pinch of ground cloves

2 teaspoons light brown soft sugar

1 teaspoon sea salt

2 teaspoons raw, unfiltered apple cider vinegar

1 tablespoon groundnut oil

300ml chicken stock, plus extra to loosen if necessary

1½ tablespoons finely ground raw cacao nibs or raw cacao powder

500g skinless, boneless chicken thighs

4–6 warmed tortillas

coriander leaves

Heat a large, dry frying pan over a medium heat and toast all the chillies in batches for 10 minutes each, turning, until they soften and develop a smoky, sweet aroma. Don't let them burn. Put the toasted chillies in a mixing bowl and cover with 250ml of just-boiled water. Press them down with a lid to submerge and soak for 20 minutes. Remove the stems and seeds and roughly chop. Reserve the soaking water. Meanwhile, soak the raisins in 100ml of just-boiled water, then drain, reserving the soaking water.

Blend the softened chillies with a splash of their soaking water, until smooth. Add the raisins, garlic, onion, tomatoes, almonds, cinnamon, allspice, cloves, sugar, salt and vinegar and blend again until smooth.

Heat the oil in a large, heavy-based casserole pan over a medium–low heat. Add the blended chilli mixture, tilting the pan away from you to prevent the hot oil or sauce spitting at you, and quickly stir to combine. Turn the heat down to low and cook part-covered for 20 minutes, stirring often. Add a splash more of the chilli soaking water if the paste looks too dry.

Take the pan off the heat. Stir in the rest of the chilli and raisin soaking waters, and add the stock. Place a sieve over a bowl, tip in the sauce and press it through the sieve with the back of a fork. Add any small bits left in the sieve to the bowl. Return the sauce to the pan and stir in the cacao.

Add the chicken and bring to the boil. Turn the heat down to low and cook, covered, for 45–60 minutes, until the chicken is cooked through and the sauce is thick. Add more stock if the sauce looks too dry. Remove from the heat, let the chicken cool a little, then remove it with a slotted spoon. Shred the chicken, then return it to the sauce. Divide the chicken mole into 4–6 equal portions and use each portion to top a warmed tortilla. Fill as below, sprinkle with coriander leaves to taste, then roll.

FILL YOUR BURRITOS

To complete your burritos, use 1 recipe quantity of:

�»→ **Coriander & Lime Rice** (see p.37)

�»→ **Charro Beans** (see p.46)

�»→ **Pico de Gallo** (see p.55)

�»→ **Roasted Pineapple Salsa** (see p.50)

YUCATÁN ACHIOTE MARINATED CHICKEN

You probably know of the Yucatán peninsula – it's that horned bit of Mexico that juts out, separating the Gulf of Mexico from the pirates of the Caribbean. It's home to lots of life, from Cancún to the quieter Tulum, and some of the most amazing food on the planet.

YOU WILL NEED

500g skinless, boneless chicken thighs

4 warmed tortillas

slices of charred (see p.26) green jalapeño chillies

FOR THE MARINADE

50g achiote paste

¾ teaspoon ground allspice

large pinch of ground cloves

1 teaspoon ground black pepper

¼ teaspoon ground cumin

4 garlic cloves, peeled

2 tablespoons vegetable oil

1 teaspoon ground coriander

1 teaspoon ground cinnamon

1½ teaspoons finely grated orange zest

3 tablespoons orange juice

1 tablespoon raw, unfiltered apple cider vinegar

To make the marinade, put all the ingredients in a mini food processor or blender and blend to a smooth paste.

Put the chicken in a non-metallic dish, spoon the marinade over and turn until the thighs are coated. Cover and leave to marinate in the fridge for 4–6 hours, or overnight if time allows – the longer, the better.

Heat a large, ridged griddle pan over a medium heat. When hot, add the chicken (you will probably need to cook it in 2 batches). Griddle the chicken for 10 minutes on each side, or until cooked through with chargrill marks, taking care not to let the marinade burn. Cut the chicken into large chunks or strips, then divide it into 4 equal portions and use each portion to top a warmed tortilla. Fill as below, sprinkle with the sliced jalapeños to taste, then roll.

FILL YOUR BURRITOS

To complete your burritos, use 1 recipe quantity of:

»→ **Coriander & Lime Rice** (see p.37)

»→ **Chipotle Black Beans** (see p.47)

»→ **Charred Jalapeño Guacamole** (see p.56)

»→ **Roasted Garlic Crema** (see p.59)

»→ **Pickled Onions** (see p.50)

CHILANGO FRIED CHICKEN

SERVES 4

Remember February 2018 when those fried-chicken bozos ran out of chicken across the entire country and had to shut their restaurants? That whole fiasco inspired us to come up with Chilango Fried Chicken (abbreviate it, you genius). Buttermilk-marinated, battered chicken tenders, with a craveable spice mix of ginger, paprika and chipotle and ancho chillies. Time to get your fried-chicken fix.

YOU WILL NEED

500g skinless, boneless, chicken thighs, cut into 2cm-thick long strips
150ml buttermilk
vegetable oil, for deep-frying
4 warmed tortillas
shredded iceberg lettuce
slices of red jalapeño chilli

FOR THE SPICE COATING

1 teaspoon ancho chilli powder
½ teaspoon ground ginger
½ teaspoon onion powder
1½ teaspoons garlic powder
1 tablespoon chipotle powder
1 tablespoon smoked paprika
½ teaspoon mustard powder
¼ teaspoon celery salt
1 tablespoon dried oregano, preferably Mexican
1 teaspoon sea salt
1 teaspoon smoked salt, preferably mesquite
1 teaspoon ground black pepper
300g plain flour

Put the chicken in a bowl. In a separate bowl, combine the buttermilk with 3 tablespoons of water and pour it over the chicken, turning to coat. Cover and marinate in the fridge for 8 hours or overnight – the longer, the better.

Just before you're ready to cook the chicken, mix together all the ingredients for the spice coating in a bowl.

Pour enough oil into a large, deep saucepan or deep-fat fryer to deep-fry the chicken. Heat the oil to 185°C/365°F, or until a cube of day-old bread turns crisp and golden in 45 seconds. Turn on the oven to low.

Working in batches, remove a piece of chicken from the buttermilk marinade, dunk it into the spiced flour and place it straight into the hot oil. Repeat to cook 4 pieces of chicken at a time. We like ours crunchy and well coated. If you want a thinner coating, give the chicken a shake to remove any excess spiced flour before frying. Deep-fry for 3–4 minutes, until golden and crisp and the chicken is cooked through. Scoop out the chicken with a slotted spoon and set aside to drain on kitchen paper. Repeat with the remaining chicken, keeping the drained, cooked strips warm in the oven. When all the chicken is cooked, divide it into 4 equal portions and use each portion to top a warmed tortilla. Fill as below, along with some shredded iceberg and some chilli slices to taste, then roll.

WHY NOT...

Go dirty: use the marinated Chilango Chicken (see p.74) to dredge through the flour and fry. You. Will. Not. Know where this has been all your life.

FILL YOUR BURRITOS

To complete your burritos, use 1 recipe quantity of:
»→ **Roasted Habanero Salsa** (see p.51)
»→ **Roasted Garlic Crema** (see p.59)
»→ **Baja Cabbage Slaw** (see p.64)

ONE-PAN ROASTED TOMATILLO CHICKEN

Tomatillos rock. They're the stars of the hot salsa verde we serve in the restaurants, and take the spotlight in this recipe. Once you shred the chicken, it will soak up all the smooth, roasted, spicy flavours from the amazing sauce.

YOU WILL NEED

250g small fresh tomatillos, diced; or 250g tinned tomatillos, drained well and chopped

4 green jalapeño chillies, deseeded and thinly sliced into rings

1 tomato, charred (see p.26), deseeded and roughly chopped

1½ teaspoons dried oregano, preferably Mexican

1 white onion, thinly sliced into rings

125ml chicken stock

2 large garlic cloves, sliced

1 tablespoon chopped tarragon leaves

1 teaspoon sea salt

1 teaspoon caster sugar

500g skinless, boneless chicken thighs

3 coriander sprigs

½ lime, for squeezing

4 warmed tortillas

grated Cheddar cheese

Preheat the oven to 150°C/300°F/Gas 2.

To make the sauce, mix together all the ingredients up to and including the sugar in a bowl. Spoon half the sauce into a 20cm ovenproof dish, then arrange the chicken on top. Spoon the remaining sauce over the chicken and add the coriander sprigs.

Cover the dish with foil, then place in the oven for 1 hour. Turn up the oven to 200°C/400°F/Gas 6. Remove the foil and bake for another 20–30 minutes, until the sauce has reduced and thickened.

Discard the coriander sprigs and remove the chicken. Shred the chicken, then return it to the sauce and squeeze over the lime juice. Divide the chicken into 4 equal portions and use each portion to top a warmed tortilla. Fill as below, sprinkle over Cheddar cheese to taste, then roll.

FILL YOUR BURRITOS

To complete your burritos, use 1 recipe quantity of:

»→ **Coriander & Lime Rice** (see p.37)

»→ **Charro Beans** (see p.46)

»→ **Tomatillo & Avocado Salsa** (see p.54)

CHARGRILLED JALAPEÑO CHICKEN

SERVES 4

Grilled. Jalapeño. Chicken. This is chicken, chargrilled, with jalapeños. What else is there to say? Simple recipe. Nice flavours.

YOU WILL NEED

500g skinless, boneless chicken breasts

4 warmed tortillas

coriander leaves

slices of charred (see p.26) green jalapeño chillies

FOR THE MARINADE

125ml vegetable oil

2 garlic cloves, crushed

30g coriander, leaves and stalks

15g flat-leaf parsley leaves

2 green jalapeño chillies, stems removed

1 tablespoon chopped oregano

finely grated zest and juice of 1 lime

1 teaspoon caster sugar

1 teaspoon sea salt

Place the chicken breasts between 2 large sheets of cling film and flatten with a meat mallet or the end of a rolling pin until about 1cm thick. Set aside.

Put all the marinade ingredients in a blender or mini food processor and blend until smooth.

Put the chicken in a non-metallic dish, spoon over the marinade and turn until coated. Cover and leave to marinate in the fridge for 1–4 hours, or overnight if time allows – the longer, the better.

Heat a large, ridged griddle pan over a medium heat. When hot, add the chicken (you will probably need to cook it in 2 batches). Griddle the chicken for 5–7 minutes on each side, until cooked through with chargrill marks, taking care not to let the marinade burn. Cut the chicken into chunky cubes or strips, dividing it into 4 equal portions. Use each portion to top a warmed tortilla. Fill as below and sprinkle with coriander leaves and slices of charred jalapeño to taste, then roll.

FILL YOUR BURRITOS

To complete your burritos, use 1 recipe quantity of:

»→ **Arroz Verde** (see p.40)

»→ **Roasted Habanero Salsa** (see p.51)

»→ **Charred Jalapeño Guacamole** (see p.56)

»→ **Crema de Comal** (see p.59)

»→ **Baja Cabbage Slaw** (see p.64)

»→ **Pickled Onions** (see p.50)

CLOCKWISE FROM TOP LEFT: **ONE-PAN ROASTED TOMATILLO CHICKEN (P.84), CHARGRILLED JALAPEÑO CHICKEN (P.85), VIETNAMESE LEMONGRASS CHICKEN (P.89), CHICKEN BIRYANI (P.88)**

CHICKEN BIRYANI

One of the things I love about burritos is that they can become a vehicle for just about any cuisine in the world. Biryani recipes layer up exotic spices and ingredients, like saffron, cardamom, aged basmati rice and dried fruits. Indian sauces often remind me of the complex flavours of Mexican moles. This is a simplified biryani recipe that you can prep in less than 30 minutes to produce a wonderfully fragrant dish in one pan. If you want to make it well ahead of time, leave out the protein until just before serving.

YOU WILL NEED

50g clarified butter or ghee

2 white onions, diced

2 garlic cloves, finely chopped

5cm piece of root ginger, grated

1 teaspoon ground turmeric

1 tablespoon medium–hot Mexican chilli powder, such as guajillo

½ teaspoon ground black pepper

½ teaspoon coriander seeds

¼ teaspoon ground cardamom

½ teaspoon ground cinnamon

4 tomatoes, diced

1 teaspoon tomato purée

1 teaspoon caster sugar

1 teaspoon sea salt

250ml chicken stock

500g skinless, boneless chicken breasts, cut into 5cm chunks

4 warmed tortillas

coriander leaves

In a large sauté pan with a lid, melt the clarified butter or ghee over a very low heat. Add the onions, garlic and ginger, cover and cook gently for 20 minutes, until soft but not coloured. Add a splash of water if the onions look dry.

Stir in the spices and cook for 1 minute, stirring, before adding the rest of the ingredients. Cover the pan and simmer gently for 20 minutes, stirring occasionally.

Add the chicken and bring the sauce up to the boil, then reduce the heat to low. Cover the pan and simmer gently without boiling for 20–25 minutes, until the chicken is cooked through. Stir occasionally to stop the sauce sticking to the bottom of the pan. Divide the chicken into 4 equal portions and use each portion to top a warmed tortilla. Fill as below, sprinkle with coriander leaves to taste, then roll.

FILL YOUR BURRITOS

To complete your burritos, use 1 recipe quantity of:

»→ **Caramelized Coconut Rice** (see p.41)

»→ **Pico de Gallo** (see p.55)

»→ **Charred Pineapple with Quick Pickled Jalapeños** (see p.153)

SERVES 4

VIETNAMESE LEMONGRASS CHICKEN

We think this marinade is perfect with chicken, but it also works well with a trimmed flank steak for a beef option.

YOU WILL NEED

500g skinless, boneless chicken
    thighs
4 warmed tortillas

FOR THE LEMONGRASS MARINADE

3 lemongrass stalks, peeled and
    roughly chopped
2 garlic cloves, crushed
1 tablespoon chopped mint leaves
1 tablespoon finely chopped serrano
    chillies or bird's eye chillies
2 shallots, diced
1 tablespoon fish sauce
75ml light soy sauce
30g palm sugar or light brown soft
    sugar
½ teaspoon ground black pepper

To make the marinade, put the lemongrass, garlic, mint, chillies and shallots in a mini food processor and blitz until finely chopped. Add the fish sauce and soy sauce and blitz again to a coarse paste. Stir in the sugar and pepper.

Put the chicken in a non-metallic dish and spoon over the lemongrass marinade. Cover and marinate in the fridge for at least 1 hour, or overnight if time allows – the longer, the better.

Preheat the oven to 180°C/350°F/Gas 4.

Heat a large, ridged griddle pan or chargrill over a high heat until very hot. Add the chicken and cook for 2 minutes on each side, until golden, then transfer to a roasting tin and place in the oven for 15–20 minutes, until cooked through. Cut the chicken into small pieces, then divide it into 4 equal portions, using each portion to top a warmed tortilla. Fill as below, then roll.

FILL YOUR BURRITOS

To complete your burritos, use 1 recipe quantity of:
- Caramelized Coconut Rice (see p.41)
- Smoky Corn Salsa (see p.50)
- Charred Pineapple with Quick Pickled Jalapeños (see p.153)
- Lime & Jalapeño Crema (see p.58)

CHICKEN AL PASTOR-STYLE

When the Lebanese settled in Mexico, they fused their shawarma spit-grilled meat with the local Mexican cuisine: tacos al pastor were born. Now, unless you take over a doner kebab shop, you'll have to make do without the vertical spit of stacked meat slices. Never fear – this recipe has the answer. Although al pastor is made with pork dishes in Mexico, we've borrowed it for this chicken burrito (and yes, it's a full-sized burrito, rather than taco).

YOU WILL NEED

500g skinless, boneless chicken thighs
4 warmed tortillas
coriander leaves
grated Cheddar cheese

FOR THE MARINADE

3 large dried guajillo chillies
1 tablespoon rapeseed oil, plus extra for frying
1 teaspoon dried oregano, preferably Mexican
1 tablespoon chipotles en adobo
125ml pineapple juice
1 red jalapeño chilli
¼ teaspoon ground allspice
1 garlic clove, peeled
1 small white onion, finely chopped
1 tablespoon raw, unfiltered apple cider vinegar
1 teaspoon caster sugar
1 teaspoon smoked salt, preferably mesquite

To make the marinade, put the guajillo chillies in a large, dry frying pan over a medium heat and toast for 2–3 minutes on each side, until they start to smell toasted. Place in a heatproof bowl and cover with just-boiled water. Press down the chillies to submerge and leave to soak for 20 minutes, until softened. Drain the chillies, then remove the stems and seeds and roughly chop. Discard the soaking water. Transfer the chopped chillies to a mini food processor or blender with the rest of the marinade ingredients and blend to a smooth paste.

Put the chicken in a non-metallic dish, spoon the marinade over and turn until the thighs are coated. Cover and leave to marinate in the fridge for 1–4 hours, or overnight if time allows – the longer, the better.

Preheat the oven to 180°C/350°F/Gas 4. Heat enough oil to cover the base of a large frying pan over a medium heat. Add the chicken thighs (you may need to cook them in 2 batches) and cook for 5 minutes on each side, until golden, occasionally spooning over some of the marinade. Transfer the chicken thighs to a roasting tin and finish off cooking them in the oven, about 15 minutes or until cooked through. Cut the chicken into chunky cubes, dividing it into 4 equal portions and using each portion to top a warmed tortilla. Fill as below, sprinkle with coriander leaves and Cheddar cheese to taste, then roll.

FILL YOUR BURRITOS

To complete your burritos, use 1 recipe quantity of:
»→ **Arroz Mexicana** (see p.37)
»→ **Charro Beans** (see p.46)
»→ **Roasted Garlic Crema** (see p.59)

BBQ CHIPOTLE CHICKEN

Chipotle sits in the top 10 of Mexican flavours, and for good reason. If you Google it you'll find that there is not necessarily one chipotle thing, but more endless variations on chipotle. It's a bit like a Ploughman's lunch in a country pub – a tad different everywhere. What you can count on is smokiness and heat; and that blended in with my personal favourite (barbecue sauce) makes you come back to this sauce again and again... and again.

YOU WILL NEED

500g skinless, boneless chicken
    thighs
vegetable oil, for cooking
4 warmed tortillas
coriander leaves

FOR THE BBQ SAUCE

2 large dried chipotle chillies
2 tablespoons raw, unfiltered,
    apple cider vinegar
75g dark brown soft sugar
75g pineapple, charred (see p.26)
2 red jalapeño chillies, charred (see
    p.26)
50g mango, charred (see p.26)
½ small onion, charred (see p.26)
2 teaspoons ground cumin
2 tablespoons Worcestershire sauce
300g tomato ketchup
1 tablespoon English mustard
finely grated zest and juice of 1 lime
½ teaspoon sea salt
½ teaspoon ground black pepper

To start the barbecue sauce, place the chipotle chillies in a heatproof bowl and cover with just-boiled water. Press down the chillies to submerge, then leave to soak for 20 minutes, until softened. Remove the stems and seeds, then roughly chop. Discard the soaking water.

Put the vinegar and sugar in a small saucepan and heat gently, stirring, until the sugar dissolves, then pour into a mixing bowl. Put the soaked chillies, pineapple, jalapeños, mango and onion in a food processor or blender and blitz to a coarse purée. Spoon into the bowl with the vinegar and sugar and stir in the rest of the sauce ingredients.

Using a sharp knife, deeply score each chicken thigh three times and place the thighs in a bowl. Spoon over half the barbecue sauce and rub it into the chicken until coated. Cover and leave to marinate in the fridge for 1 hour.

Preheat the oven to 180°C/350°F/Gas 4. Heat a large, ridged griddle pan or chargrill over a high heat. Add a splash of oil, then reduce the heat to medium. Add the chicken, discarding the marinade, and griddle for 5 minutes on each side, until golden. Transfer the chicken to a roasting tin and place in the oven for 10–15 minutes, or until cooked through.

Pour the rest of the barbecue sauce in a small saucepan, add a splash of water to loosen and warm through. Slather as much of the barbecue sauce over the chicken as you like. Cut the chicken into small pieces, dividing it into 4 equal portions and using each portion to top a warmed tortilla. Fill as below, sprinkle with coriander leaves to taste, then roll.

FILL YOUR BURRITOS

To complete your burritos, use 1 recipe quantity of:

»→ **Coriander & Lime Rice** (see p.37)
»→ **Classic Guacamole** (see p.56)
»→ **Chipotle Crema** (see p.58)

THIS PAGE: **CHICKEN AL PASTOR-STYLE (P.90)**
OPPOSITE: **BBQ CHIPOTLE CHICKEN (P.91)**

EL JEFFE

El Jeffe ("The Boss") is like the Mario Brothers end-boss of burritos – two burritos rolled together, a monster. To make this bad boy, you overlap one tortilla by a quarter-circle with another and then you fill the whole lot and roll as one. We've added spice, because if you're big enough to eat this, you're big enough to handle your heat. Here's what goes in: 1 full recipe quantity of Chilango Chicken (p.74), Roasted Habanero Salsa (p.51), Spicy Chilli Rice (p.36) and Chipotle Black Beans (p.47), Chipotle Crema (p.58) and Pickled Onion (p.50), along with some shredded iceberg lettuce and sliced red jalapeño chilli. Respect.

CHICKEN 14

Why do we call this Chicken 14? Because we needed 14 recipes to finish the section, and this is the 14th recipe. All hail Chicken 14. Seriously, though, you're gonna love this one. One big succulent chicken, stuffed with lemons and jalapeños, and doused liberally with a can of beer and a double shot of tequila. Shred the chicken at the end to soak up every last bit of the sauce.

YOU WILL NEED

1 whole chicken without giblets
    (about 1.6kg)
1 lemon, quartered
3 green or red jalapeño chillies, split
    lengthways
33cl can Corona or other lager or IPA
double shot of tequila, about
    4 tablespoons
40g cold unsalted butter
4–6 warmed tortillas

FOR THE MARINADE

1 teaspoon onion powder
1 teaspoon garlic powder
1 teaspoon ground ginger
1 teaspoon smoked salt, preferably
    mesquite
1 teaspoon ground allspice
½ teaspoon cinnamon
2 teaspoons smoked paprika
2 teaspoons dried thyme
1 teaspoon ground black pepper
1½ teaspoons chipotle powder
2 teaspoons chicken stock powder
5 tablespoons vegetable oil

Mix together all the ingredients for the marinade. Put the chicken in a shallow dish, brush the marinade all over the chicken, cover and leave in the fridge to marinate overnight.

Preheat the oven to 180°C/350°F/Gas 4. Stuff the lemon and chillies into the chicken cavity. Open the can of lager and pour out half, reserving to make the gravy later. Put the can in the middle of a roasting tray and position the chicken on top, pushing it down to insert the can into the chicken cavity, so the chicken sits upright on the can. Brush the chicken all over with more marinade.

Roast the chicken for 1 hour 20 minutes, basting it every 20 minutes with the juices in the tray, until cooked through, golden and the juices run clear when the thickest part of the thigh is pierced with a skewer. Remove the chicken from the tray, carefully lifting it off the can. Place the chicken on a warm plate, cover with foil and leave to rest while you make the gravy.

Strain the cooking juices from the tray into a saucepan, skimming off any oil sitting on the top. Add the beer left in the can as well as the reserved beer and the tequila. Bring to the boil, then simmer until there is no aroma of alcohol and the sauce has reduced by half, about 10 minutes – it's quite a light, boozy gravy. Remove from the heat and stir in the butter. Brush the gravy over the chicken before shredding or slicing. Stir the sliced or shredded chicken through the remaining gravy to soak it up. Divide into 4–6 equal portions and use each to top a warmed tortilla. Fill as below, then roll. (Or, slice the chicken and serve with the gravy and no burrito at all.)

FILL YOUR BURRITOS

To complete your burritos, use 1 recipe quantity of:
»→ **Coriander & Lime Rice** (see p.37)
»→ **Chipotle Black Beans** (see p.47)
»→ **Roasted Habanero Salsa** (see p.51)
»→ **Roasted Garlic Crema** (see p.59)
»→ **Pickled Onions** (see p.50)

BEEF

WHERE'S THE BEEF? IF YOU KNOW WHERE THAT PHRASE ORIGINATES FROM YOU GET A MASSIVE +1. ANYWAY, IT'S TIME TO REJOICE, FOR THY BEEF HATH COMETH. THERE'S A LOT OF FLAVOUR ACROSS THE PAGES THAT FOLLOW, BUT TWO OF THE RECIPES ARE PARTICULARLY MIND-BLOWING. ENTER BARBACOA BEEF AND THE BRAISED SHORT RIBS. ADVANCED WARNING: THESE ARE NOT THE EASIEST BEEF FILLINGS TO MAKE AND TAKE A LITTLE MORE EFFORT THAN THE OTHERS, BUT IF YOU'RE UP FOR THE CHALLENGE, TREASURE AWAITS.

BBQ BRAISED BEEF BRISKET

SERVES 6

If you're a hipster you've been cooking brisket since 2010. Probably low and slow over some Bourbon-infused flaked cherrywood. The craze for it started in the USA and then came to the UK; but, of course, a brisket in America is a different cut to the UK. Why wouldn't it be, huh? Some retailers have adopted whichever one they could get their mitts on. To you that doesn't make too much difference as ultimately it's the BBQ sauce in this recipe that will make you punch the air.

YOU WILL NEED

1 teaspoon smoked salt, preferably mesquite

1 tablespoon chipotle powder

½ teaspoon ground black pepper

1kg beef brisket, fat trimmed, meat cut into 6 large pieces

2 tablespoons vegetable oil

6 warmed tortillas

coriander leaves

slices of red jalapeño chilli

FOR THE BBQ BEEF SAUCE

250g BBQ Sauce (see p.91)

30g chipotles en adobo

3 garlic cloves, dry roasted (see p.26)

140g tomatoes, charred (see p.26)

1 teaspoon Tabasco chipotle sauce

1 teaspoon liquid smoke

1 small onion, diced

Mix together the smoked salt, chipotle powder and black pepper. Put the brisket in a bowl, add the smoked salt mix and turn the meat to coat.

Put all the ingredients for the BBQ Beef Sauce in a blender with 300ml of water and blend until smooth. Set aside.

Preheat the oven to 130°C/250°F/Gas 1. Heat half the oil in a large heavy-based casserole over a high heat. Add half the beef and cook until browned all over, about 5 minutes. Using tongs, transfer the beef to a bowl. Add more oil to the pan, if needed, and the rest of the beef, and brown for 5 minutes.

Return the first batch of beef to the pan with the sauce and turn to coat the meat. Bring to the boil, then cover with a lid and place in the oven for 3 hours, occasionally checking that it is not drying out. Add a splash of water, if needed. Leave the beef to rest for 20 minutes.

Lift out the beef from the sauce onto a plate. Roughly shred the meat into long strands, then spoon the sauce over. Divide the beef into 6 equal portions, using each portion to top a warmed tortilla. Fill as below and sprinkle with coriander leaves and chilli slices to taste, then roll.

FILL YOUR BURRITOS

To complete your burritos, use 1 recipe quantity of:

»→ Arroz Verde (see p.40)

»→ Pico de Gallo (see p.55)

»→ Roasted Pineapple Salsa (see p.50)

SERVES 6

BARBACOA BEEF

This one is going to blow up your mouth with flavour. It's one of the more complex recipes to make, but the hard work will pay off handsomely.

YOU WILL NEED

1 dried chipotle chilli

400g plum tomatoes, charred (see p.26), or use a 400g tin

1kg beef brisket, fat trimmed, meat cut into 6 large pieces

3 tablespoons vegetable oil

1½ teaspoons sea salt

1 litre beef stock

2 onions, chopped

1 bay leaf

30g chipotles en adobo, chopped

2 red jalapeño chillies, diced, plus extra slices to roll

1 tablespoon thyme leaves

2 tablespoons tomato purée

2 garlic cloves, crushed

½ teaspoon ground cinnamon

1 tablespoon oregano leaves

½ teaspoon allspice

½ teaspoon ground cumin

1 teaspoon liquid smoke

3 tablespoons raw, unfiltered apple cider vinegar

ground black pepper

6 warmed tortillas

coriander leaves

Place the chipotle in a heatproof bowl and cover with just-boiled water. Press down to submerge, then leave it to soak for 20 minutes, until softened. Drain, remove the stem and seeds and finely chop. Set aside.

Meanwhile, blitz the tomatoes in a blender to a coarse purée and set aside.

Preheat the oven to 130°C/250°F/Gas 1. Put the beef in a bowl, then add 2 tablespoons of the oil and sprinkle over the salt. Turn the meat to coat. Heat a large heavy-based casserole pan over a high heat until smoking. Add half the beef and cook until browned all over, about 5 minutes. Using tongs, transfer the beef to a large bowl. Add the remaining beef to the pan and brown for 5 minutes. Put the second batch of beef in the bowl and deglaze the pan with a third of the stock, stirring to remove any bits stuck to the bottom of the pan. Pour the stock into the bowl with the beef.

Turn the heat to medium–low and add the remaining oil to the casserole. Add the onions and sauté for 8 minutes, or until lightly coloured and translucent. Add the soaked chipotles and the remaining ingredients, except the blended tomatoes and the remaining stock, and cook for 3 minutes. Stir in the tomatoes and cook for 2 minutes more, then add the remaining stock, browned beef and deglazed juices and bring to the boil. Cover with a lid and place in the oven for 3–4 hours, checking the liquid level every hour and giving a stir, until the meat is tender.

Lift the beef from the sauce onto a plate. Reduce the sauce over a medium–high heat for 20 minutes, or until reduced by two-thirds. Meanwhile, shred the beef. Blend the reduced sauce to a smooth purée, then return the beef to the sauce and turn until combined. Divide the beef into 6 equal portions and use each portion to top a warmed tortilla. Fill as below, sprinkle with coriander leaves and the extra slices of jalapeño chilli to taste, then roll.

FILL YOUR BURRITOS

To complete your burritos, use 1 recipe quantity of:

»→ **Arroz Verde** (see p.40)

»→ **Roasted Pineapple Salsa** (see p.50)

»→ **Pickled Onions** (see p.50)

»→ **Lime & Jalapeño Crema** (see p.58), optional

STEAK FAJITAS

This dish reminds me of growing up. Not that we'd cook it at home, but when we'd hit up some Mexican joint while out for a meal, steak fajitas always made their way onto the table. I always think the cumin, chipotle and paprika, together with a squeeze of fresh lime, are the stand-out flavours here. The key thing is to char the vegetables, but not cook them so much that they lose their crispness.

YOU WILL NEED

2 tablespoons rapeseed oil

2 x 225–350g sirloin steaks, patted dry, fat trimmed, meat cut into 2cm-thick slices

1 large white onion, halved and sliced

1 large red pepper, deseeded and thinly sliced into long strips

1 large yellow pepper, deseeded and thinly sliced into long strips

1 large green pepper, deseeded and thinly sliced into long strips

1 lime, for squeezing

4 warmed tortillas

shredded iceberg lettuce leaves

grated Cheddar cheese

FOR THE FAJITA SPICE MIX

1½ teaspoons smoked salt, preferably mesquite

½ teaspoon ground black pepper

½ teaspoon garlic powder

½ teaspoon onion powder

2 teaspoons smoked paprika

½ teaspoon ground cumin

1 teaspoon chipotle powder

½ teaspoon dried oregano, preferably Mexican

½ teaspoon light brown soft sugar

Mix together all the ingredients for the fajita spice mix.

Mix 2 tablespoons of the spice mix with half the oil in a large, shallow bowl. Add the steak and rub the mixture into the meat, then leave to marinate and come up to room temperature, about 30 minutes.

Meanwhile, put the onion and all the peppers in a large bowl. Pour over the remaining oil and fajita spice mix and toss until combined.

Heat a large, ridged griddle pan or chargrill over a high heat until hot. Chargrill the vegetables in batches for about 3 minutes per batch, turning them occasionally until they are charred in places but retain their crunch. Take care not to overload the pan – the vegetables need space, otherwise they will steam rather than chargrill. When cooked, put the vegetables in a bowl, squeeze over the lime juice and cover to keep warm.

Wipe the griddle pan or chargrill clean with kitchen paper, then return it to a high heat. Add the steak slices and sear for 1½–2 minutes on each side, or until cooked to your liking. Remove to a warm plate, cover and leave to rest for 5 minutes. Divide the steak into 4 equal portions, using each portion to top a warmed tortilla. Add the charred vegetables and sauces (see below), along with some shredded iceberg lettuce and cheese to taste.

FILL YOUR FAJITAS

To complete your fajitas, use 1 recipe quantity of:
- Roasted Habanero Salsa (see p.51)
- Charred Jalapeño Guacamole (see p.56)

CLOCKWISE FROM TOP LEFT: **BARBACOA BEEF (P.102),
BRAISED SHORT RIBS (P.106), CHIMICHURRI STEAK
(P.107), STEAK FAJITAS (P.103)**

BRAISED SHORT RIBS

Another flavour bomb – and if you only ever make this recipe and the Barbacoa Beef on page 102, so be it. You won't regret one minute of time and effort you spend on this beef. And your guests will think you're a god. The recipe officially serves four but, frankly, double up – it will still serve four.

YOU WILL NEED

1½ tablespoons vegetable oil

4–6 meaty beef short ribs

350ml pale ale

1 tomato, roughly chopped

40g tomato purée

200g chipotles en adobo, chopped

1 tablespoon tamarind paste

5 garlic cloves, dry roasted (see p.26), chopped

finely grated zest of 1 orange

25g dark brown soft sugar

1 teaspoon ground allspice

1 bay leaf

2 teaspoons dried thyme

350ml double-strength beef stock

4 warmed tortillas

shredded iceberg lettuce leaves

grated Cheddar cheese

Heat a large, heavy-based casserole pan over a high heat until smoking. Add the oil and half the beef ribs and cook until browned all over, about 5 minutes. Using tongs, transfer the ribs to a plate. Add the remaining ribs to the pan and brown for 5 minutes. Place the second batch of beef on the plate and deglaze the pan with the ale, stirring to remove any bits stuck to the bottom of the pan.

Preheat the oven to 150°C/300°F/Gas 2.

Add the tomato, tomato purée, chipotles en adobo, tamarind paste, garlic, orange zest, sugar, allspice, bay leaf, thyme and beef stock, stir well and bring to the boil. Return the ribs to the casserole or transfer to a roasting tin and pour the sauce over. Turn the ribs to coat them in the sauce, cover the pan with a lid or the tin with foil. Roast for 3½–4 hours, checking every so often there is enough liquid in the pan or tin and adding a splash of water if needed, until the beef is tender and just falling away from the bone.

Lift out the ribs onto a plate, cover with foil and leave to rest while you reduce the sauce. Place the pan or tin on a hob over a medium–high heat, skimming off any fat on the surface. Let the sauce bubble away for 15 minutes, or until reduced by half. While the sauce is reducing, shred the beef into long strands, discarding the bones. Once the sauce has reduced, return the beef to the pan and turn until combined. Divide the beef into 4 equal portions and use each portion to top a warmed tortilla. Fill as below, add lettuce and cheese to taste, then roll.

FILL YOUR BURRITOS

To complete your burritos, use 1 recipe quantity of:

→ **Spicy Chilli Rice** (see p.36)

→ **Tomatillo & Avocado Salsa** (see p.54)

→ **Lime & Jalapeño Crema** (see p.58) or **Chipotle Crema** (see p.58)

→ **Pickled Onions** (see p.50)

CHIMICHURRI STEAK

Try this one when you're in a jam. It's quick and gets the job done. The herbs, lemon zest, garlic and chillies are the highlights.

YOU WILL NEED

1 tablespoon rapeseed oil

2 x 225–350g sirloin steaks, patted dry

4 warmed tortillas

grated Cheddar cheese

FOR THE CHIMICHURRI SAUCE

1 handful of flat-leaf parsley

1 handful of oregano leaves

1 handful of mint leaves

generous ½ bunch of dill sprigs

1 teaspoon finely grated lemon zest

2 garlic cloves, crushed

2 red or green bird's eye chillies, deseeded

1 tablespoon white wine vinegar

4 tablespoons olive oil

1 teaspoon sea salt, plus extra for seasoning the oil

¼ teaspoon ground black pepper, plus extra for seasoning the oil

Season the oil with salt and pepper and rub the mixture all over both sides of each steak. Set aside to come to room temperature, about 20–30 minutes.

To make the chimichurri sauce, put the herbs, lemon zest, garlic and chillies in a food processor and pulse to a coarse purée. Stir in the remaining ingredients and set aside.

Heat a large, ridged griddle pan or chargrill over a high heat until hot. Add the steaks and sear for 1½–2 minutes on each side, or until cooked to your liking. Remove from the heat to a warm plate, cover and leave to rest for 5 minutes. Slice the steak into 2cm-thick strips, divide it into 4 equal portions and use each portion to top a warmed tortilla. Fill as below, then scatter over the cheese to taste, drizzle over a little chimichurri sauce, and roll. Serve with any remaining sauce on the side.

FILL YOUR BURRITOS

To complete your burritos, use 1 recipe quantity of:

»→ Coriander & Lime Rice (see p.37)

»→ Charred Pineapple with Quick Pickled Jalapeños (see p.153)

»→ Pickled Onions (see p.50)

CHARGRILLED THAI STEAK WITH PINEAPPLE SALSA

I love Thai food as much as Mexican. Maybe someday I'll open a Thai joint. The combination of mushrooms, pineapples and chillies with the Thai basil will bring some Southeast Asian vibrancy to your Latin dinner table. Get that pineapple charring and it'll feel like you're eating burritos on the beaches of Phuket.

YOU WILL NEED

300g peeled pineapple, cut into 1cm-thick rings

2 x 225–350g sirloin steaks, patted dry

1 ripe Hass avocado, halved, stoned and flesh diced

6 shiitake mushrooms, stems removed, cups sliced

4 warmed tortillas

coriander leaves

FOR THE THAI MARINADE

2 tablespoons rapeseed oil, plus extra for cooking the mushrooms

2 large lemongrass stalks, peeled and finely chopped

1 tablespoon sambal oelek

1 shallot, finely chopped

1 teaspoon finely chopped galangal

2 teaspoons finely chopped ginger root

½ teaspoon finely chopped garlic

2 fresh kaffir lime leaves, thinly sliced

1 tablespoon fish sauce

4 teaspoons kicap manis (sweet soy sauce)

1 tablespoon sliced Thai basil or regular basil

1 tablespoon finely chopped coriander leaves

2 tablespoons light soy sauce

Place the pineapple in a large, dry frying pan and gently caramelize over a medium–low heat for about 4–5 minutes on each side, until light golden in places. Make sure that it doesn't darken too much, otherwise it will taste burnt. Remove from the pan and cut into small dice, discarding the core.

Put all the ingredients for the Thai marinade in a mini food processor or blender with a third of the charred pineapple and blitz to a coarse purée.

Put the steaks in a non-metallic dish, spoon over two-thirds of the marinade and rub it into the steaks to coat all over. Cover and leave to marinate at room temperature for 1 hour.

Meanwhile, mix the remaining marinade with the rest of the pineapple, the avocado and 2 tablespoons of water and set aside.

Heat a large, ridged griddle pan or chargrill over a high heat until hot. Add the steaks and sear for 1½–2 minutes on each side, or until cooked to your liking. Remove from the heat to a warm plate, cover and leave to rest for 5 minutes while you cook the mushrooms. Toss the mushrooms in a little oil and chargrill for 5 minutes, turning once, until tender.

Cut the steaks into 2cm slices. Divide into 4 equal portions and use each portion to top a warmed tortilla. Add the mushrooms and the pineapple salsa (alternatively, you can serve these on the side), fill as below, sprinkle with coriander leaves to taste, then roll.

FILL YOUR BURRITOS

To complete your burritos, use 1 recipe quantity of:

»→ **Arroz Verde** (see p.40)

»→ **Smoky Corn Salsa** (see p.50)

ULTIMATE SURF 'N' TURF

When it comes to burritos, this is the pinnacle, the ultimate indulgence. Flambé a large, thin Wagyu steak in tequila butter (a large knob of butter to 6 tablespoons of tequila should do it), then slice (it needs no other cooking). Then, build your burrito on a warmed tortilla from the bottom up: Spicy Chilli Rice (p.36), Lobster in Basil & Chipotle Butter (p.143), Tomatillo & Avocado Salsa (p.54), Pickled Onions (p.50), and finally the sliced Wagyu and a smattering of sliced charred green jalapeño chillies. Enjoy.

GRILLED STEAK TAMPIQUEÑA

Borrowed from one of Mexico's most popular meat dishes, *carne a la tampiqueña* originated in the eastern port city of Tampico. The super-simple marinade takes your tenderized steaks up a notch.

YOU WILL NEED

2 x 225–350g sirloin steaks, patted dry
splash of vegetable oil
4 warmed tortillas
coriander leaves

FOR THE MARINADE

½ teaspoon coriander seeds
2 tablespoons lime juice
¾ teaspoon smoked salt, preferably mesquite
1 tablespoon finely grated white onion
2 large garlic cloves, crushed

First flatten the steaks slightly using a meat mallet or the end of a rolling pin until they are about 2cm thick.

To make the marinade, first toast the coriander seeds. Put them in a dry frying pan over a medium heat and toast for 1–2 minutes, until they smell aromatic. Grind in a pestle and mortar to a powder, or use a grinder.

Mix together all the ingredients for the marinade, including the ground coriander seeds. Liberally brush the marinade over the steaks, cover and leave to marinate at room temperature for 1 hour.

Heat a large, ridged griddle pan or chargrill over a high heat until hot. Brush with oil, then add the steaks and sear for 1 minute on each side, or until cooked to your liking. Remove from the heat to a warm plate, cover and leave to rest for 5 minutes. Cut into 1cm-thick slices, then divide into 4 equal portions, using each portion to top a warmed tortilla. Fill as below, sprinkle over the coriander leaves to taste, then roll.

FILL YOUR BURRITOS

To complete your burritos, use 1 recipe quantity of:
»→ **Spicy Chilli Rice** (see p.36)
»→ **Roasted Pineapple Salsa** (see p.50)
»→ **Chipotle Crema** (see p.58)

CARNE ASADA

This marinated steak is really making the meco and cascabel chillies sing without blowing your socks off. You get a nice background heat that showcases the quality of these weird-looking, leathery chillies. Soak them to bring them back to life. This recipe is a killer for a summer barbecue. Keep basting that steak until you've finished cooking.

YOU WILL NEED

2 x 225–350g sirloin steaks, patted dry
4 warmed tortillas
coriander leaves
slices of red jalapeño chilli

FOR THE MARINADE

15g dried chipotle meco chilli (about 2 chillies)
1 dried cascabel chilli
1½ teaspoons cumin seeds
150g tomatoes, charred (see p.26), deseeded and chopped
4 garlic cloves
juice of ½ lime
finely grated zest of 1 lime
2 large red chillies, roughly chopped
1 tablespoon vegetable oil, plus extra for cooking
1 teaspoon sea salt
½ teaspoon ground black pepper

To make the marinade, place the meco and cascabel chillies in a heatproof bowl and cover with just-boiled water. Press the chillies down to submerge, and leave to soak for 20 minutes, until softened. Drain, then remove the stem and seeds and roughly chop. Discard the soaking water.

While the chillies are soaking, put the cumin seeds in a dry frying pan over a medium heat and toast for 1–2 minutes, until they smell aromatic. Grind in a pestle and mortar to a powder, or use a grinder.

Transfer the soaked chillies and the cumin seeds to a mini food processor or blender with the rest of the marinade ingredients and blend to the consistency of runny ketchup.

Spoon the marinade over the steaks, cover and leave to marinate at room temperature for 1 hour, or longer in the fridge if you have time.

Heat a large, ridged griddle pan or chargrill over a high heat until hot. Brush the pan with oil, add the steaks and sear for 1½ minutes on each side, or until cooked to your liking, occasionally basting them with the marinade. Remove from the heat to a warm plate, cover and leave to rest for 5 minutes. Cut into 1cm-thick slices, then divide into 4 equal portions, using each portion to top a warmed tortilla. Fill as below, sprinkle over the coriander leaves and chilli slices to taste, then roll.

FILL YOUR BURRITOS

To complete your burritos, use 1 recipe quantity of:
»→ **Coriander & Lime Rice** (see p.37)
»→ **Chipotle Black Beans** (see p.47)
»→ **Salsa Verde** (see p.55)
»→ **Chipotle Crema** (see p.58)

THIS PAGE: **GRILLED STEAK TAMPIQUEÑA (P.112)**
OPPOSITE: **CARNE ASADA (P.113)**

PORK

IF YOU MAKE YOUR WAY TO MEXICO, ONE OF THE
THINGS YOU'LL FIND FRONT AND CENTRE IS PORK,
IN JUST ABOUT EVERY FASHION IMAGINABLE. WE
CERTAINLY CAN'T GIVE THE FULL RANGE OF MEXICAN
OPTIONS JUSTICE IN JUST THE FEW PAGES OF THIS
CHAPTER, BUT YOU'LL FIND A NICE COLLECTION OF
TASTY FAVOURITES. IF YOU'RE LIKE US, YOU START
TO SALIVATE WHEN YOU SEE WORDS AND PHRASES
LIKE "CHORIZO" AND "BBQ PULLED PORK", SO DON'T
READ TOO LONG BEFORE YOU JUST GET GOING AND
START COOKING.

STICKY CHORIZO

Who doesn't love chorizo? For this recipe make sure you buy some decent cooking chorizo sausages. The spicy ones made by Brindisa (see p.191) are to die for; alternatively, get some through the butcher. Some supermarket offerings are laden with too much fat and additives that chorizo just doesn't need.

YOU WILL NEED

4 large cooking chorizo sausages

4 teaspoons maple syrup

6 tablespoons BBQ Sauce (see p.91)

4 warmed tortillas

finely chopped coriander leaves

Preheat the oven to 180°C/350°F/Gas 4.

Heat a large, ridged griddle pan or chargrill over a high heat until smoking. Add the chorizo sausages and cook for 4 minutes, turning them until there are char lines all over.

Transfer the sausages to a roasting tray and brush all over with the maple syrup. Roast for 15 minutes, turning once, until cooked. Toss the sausages in the barbecue sauce until coated.

Heat the grill to high. Flash the sausages under the grill for 30 seconds, turning once, or until the sauce starts to caramelize. Slice the sausages into rounds, then divide into 4 equal portions, using each portion to top a warmed tortilla. Fill as below, sprinkle over the chopped coriander leaves to taste, then roll.

FILL YOUR BURRITOS

To complete your burritos, use 1 recipe quantity of:

→ **Arroz Mexicana** (see p.37)

→ **Chipotle Black Beans** (see p.47)

→ **Roasted Pineapple Salsa** (see p.50)

→ **Charred Jalapeño Guacamole** (see p.56)

PORK MONDONGO

This vibrant green stew is Spanish in origin, but found across Latin America. We're using pork shoulder instead of the traditional tripe, to ensure you actually want to make and eat it. Shoulder is still a cheap cut, so get it quick before some chef makes it the next flat-iron steak.

YOU WILL NEED

3 tablespoons vegetable oil

550g pork shoulder, fat trimmed and meat cut into bite-sized chunks

300g cooking chorizo, sliced

1 large onion, cut into chunks and charred (see p.26)

1 large yellow pepper, deseeded and cut into large chunks

1 large red pepper, deseeded and cut into large chunks

2 carrots, cut into chunks

3–5 green jalapeño chillies, charred (see p.26) and sliced

4 large garlic cloves, crushed

1 teaspoon ground cumin

2 teaspoons smoked paprika

1 teaspoon chipotle powder

½ teaspoon ground allspice

800g tomatoes, charred (see p.26) and chopped

1 teaspoon thyme leaves

1 bunch of coriander, leaves and stalks separated, then each chopped

1 teaspoon sea salt

½ teaspoon ground black pepper

1 tablespoon agave syrup or nectar

4 teaspoons lime juice

4–6 warmed tortillas

Heat half the oil in a large, heavy-based casserole pan over a high heat. Add the pork and cook for about 5 minutes, until browned all over. You may need to cook it in 2 batches. Using tongs, transfer the pork to a large bowl. Add the chorizo to the pan and cook for about 5 minutes, until browned, then place in the bowl with the pork.

Turn the heat down to medium–low and add the rest of the oil to the casserole. Add the charred onion and fry for 3 minutes, then add all the peppers and the carrot and jalapeño and cook for another 5 minutes, until softened. Stir in the garlic and spices and return the pork and chorizo to the pan.

Next, purée the charred tomatoes and add them to the pan with 300ml of water, the thyme leaves and the coriander stalks and bring to the boil. Turn the heat down to low, part-cover, and simmer for 2 hours, stirring occasionally, until the pork is tender. Remove the lid to reduce the sauce if necessary, or cover with the lid if the pork is drying out.

Just before serving, stir in the salt, pepper, agave and lime juice. Divide the pork into 4–6 equal portions and use each to top a warmed tortilla. Fill as below, sprinkle over the coriander leaves to taste, then roll.

FILL YOUR BURRITOS

To complete your burritos, use 1 recipe quantity of:

»→ **Coriander & Lime Rice** (see p.37)

»→ **Smoky Corn Salsa** (see p.50)

»→ **Roasted Garlic Crema** (see p.59)

»→ **Pickled Onions** (see p.50)

CLOCKWISE FROM TOP LEFT: **STICKY CHORIZO (P.118), PORK MONDONGO (P.119), PORK CARNITAS (P.123), SLOW-COOKED BBQ PULLED PORK (P.122)**

SLOW-COOKED BBQ PULLED PORK

Pulled pork is to burritos as tequila is to margaritas. The pulled pork may take a while to cook, but the results are so right, the wait is totally worth it.

YOU WILL NEED

750g skinless, boneless pork shoulder, excess fat trimmed and meat cut into 4 large chunks

1 teaspoon sea salt

3 tablespoons vegetable oil

700ml double-strength chicken stock

1 large white onion, finely chopped

1 bay leaf

1 teaspoon thyme leaves

1 teaspoon dried oregano, preferably Mexican

1 teaspoon liquid smoke

2 garlic cloves, finely chopped

2 tablespoons chipotles en adobo

40g tomato purée

2 teaspoons smoked paprika

¼ teaspoon ground cinnamon

¼ teaspoon ground allspice

½ teaspoon ground black pepper

1 teaspoon ground cumin

1 tablespoon dark brown soft sugar

500ml pineapple juice

2 teaspoons raw, unfiltered apple cider vinegar

100ml thick soured cream

4 warmed tortillas

1 lime, for squeezing

coriander leaves

In a large bowl, mix together the pork, salt and 1 tablespoon of the oil.

Heat a large, heavy-based casserole pan over a high heat. Add half the pork and cook for about 5 minutes, until browned all over. Using tongs, transfer the pork to a bowl. Add another tablespoon of the oil to the pan, then the remaining pork, and repeat. Combine the 2 batches of pork and set aside.

Pour a third of the stock into the pan and deglaze, stirring to make sure you scrape up all the sticky bits, then add to the bowl with the pork.

Turn the heat down to medium, add the remaining oil to the pan with the onion and cook for 7 minutes, until soft and translucent. Add the herbs, liquid smoke, garlic, chipotles, purée and all the spices and cook for another 3 minutes, stirring occasionally.

Preheat the oven to 130°C/250°F/Gas 1. Pour the rest of the stock into the pan and add the sugar, pineapple juice and vinegar. Bring to the boil, then add the pork. Cover with a lid and place in the oven for 3 hours, occasionally checking that it is not drying out. Add a splash of water, if needed.

Lift out the pork from the sauce into a bowl and roughly shred into long strips. Cover and leave to rest while you reduce the sauce.

Place the pan on the hob and let it bubble away for about 20 minutes, or until reduced by a third. Using a hand blender, blend the sauce until smooth. Spoon 100ml of the sauce into a bowl with the soured cream to make a crema. Spoon the rest of the sauce over the pork. Divide the pork into 4 equal portions and use each portion to top a warmed tortilla. Fill as below, sprinkle over the pork crema and a good squeeze of lime juice, and some coriander leaves to taste, then roll. Hello...

FILL YOUR BURRITOS

To complete your burritos, use 1 recipe quantity of:

»→ **Arroz Verde** (see p.40)

»→ **Roasted Habanero Salsa** (see p.51)

»→ **Pickled Onions** (see p.50)

PORK CARNITAS

SERVES 4–6

Sink your teeth into our take on pork carnitas. The overnight marinade does wonders, really making the flavours shine. When you're finishing things off, make sure you use every last bit of the sauce.

YOU WILL NEED

800g pork shoulder, fat trimmed and meat cut into 4 pieces

2 teaspoons dried thyme

20g light brown soft sugar

2 teaspoons sea salt

1 tablespoon dried oregano, preferably Mexican

2 teaspoons ground cumin

1 tablespoon smoked paprika

½ teaspoon ground black pepper

4–6 warmed tortillas

finely chopped coriander leaves

FOR THE SAUCE

3 large dried ancho chillies

1 Scotch bonnet chilli, deseeded

1 bay leaf

2 garlic cloves, dry roasted (see p.26)

juice of 2 limes

100ml orange juice

2 green jalapeño chillies, charred (see p.26)

1 small onion, charred (see p.26)

300g tomatoes, charred (see p.26)

Put the pork in a large, heavy-based casserole. Mix together the thyme, sugar, salt, oregano, cumin, smoked paprika and pepper and rub the mixture all over the pork. Cover and leave the pork to marinate in the fridge overnight. An hour or so before you are ready to cook the pork, remove it from the fridge to bring it to room temperature.

Preheat the oven to 150°C/300°F/Gas 2.

Make the sauce. Put the ancho chillies in a small pan, cover with water, place over a high heat and bring to the boil. Boil for 10 minutes, or until the chillies are rehydrated and tender. Remove the chillies from the water using a slotted spoon and remove the stems but not the seeds. Reserve 100ml of the cooking water. Put all the ingredients for the sauce, including the soaked ancho chillies and the reserved cooking water, in a blender and blend until smooth.

Add enough of the sauce to cover the rubbed pork and turn until combined. (You should have about half the sauce left over.) Heat the pork over a medium heat, until the sauce reaches boiling point, then place in the oven for 2½–3 hours, until the pork is tender. Lift the pork out of the pan onto a board and shred. Spoon over enough of the sauce to coat generously. Divide the pork into 4–6 equal portions and use each portion to top a warmed tortilla. Fill as below, sprinkle over chopped coriander leaves to taste, then roll.

FILL YOUR BURRITOS

To complete your burritos, use 1 recipe quantity of:

»→ **Arroz Mexicana** (see p.37)

»→ **Refried Chipotle Black Beans** (see p.47)

»→ **Smoky Corn Salsa** (see p.50)

»→ **Red Taquería Salsa** (see p.54)

PORCHETTA

This recipe makes a stop in beautiful Italy. A rolled pork belly, slow cooked, then Mexed up for the occasion with chipotle.

YOU WILL NEED

1.3kg pork belly, skin scored

1 teaspoon sea salt

4 warmed tortillas

FOR THE MARINADE

20g chipotles en adobo, chopped

1 teaspoon chipotle powder

¼ teaspoon ground cinnamon

½ teaspoon ground black pepper

1 teaspoon dried thyme

1 teaspoon smoked salt, preferably mesquite

1 teaspoon smoked paprika

2 red jalapeño chillies, charred (see p.26) and deseeded

3 garlic cloves, dry roasted (see p.26)

Preheat the oven to its highest setting. Pour just-boiled water from a kettle over the skin of the pork, then drain the meat and pat dry with kitchen paper. Rub the salt into the skin.

Blend the marinade ingredients together in a food processor or mini blender to make a coarse paste, then rub it into the meat side of the pork. Roll the pork tightly and tie with kitchen string, then place in a roasting tin.

Roast the pork for 10 minutes, then turn the pork over and cook the other side for a further 10 minutes, until the skin is evenly crisp. Reduce the heat to 170°C/325°F/Gas 3 and continue to cook for a further 2½ hours. Remove the pork from the tin, cover and leave to rest for 15 minutes.

If you want to crisp up the skin to make crackling, turn the oven up to 200°C/400°F/Gas 6. Remove the string from the pork, slice off the skin and return it to the roasting tin. Roast until the skin is crisp and golden, about 10 minutes. Meanwhile, slice the pork meat and divide it into 4 equal portions, using each portion to top a warmed tortilla. Fill as below, then roll. Serve the crackling on the side, if you wish.

FILL YOUR BURRITOS

To complete your burritos, use 1 recipe quantity of:

»→ **Coriander & Lime Rice** (see p.37)

»→ **Chipotle Black Beans** (see p.47)

»→ **Pico de Gallo** (see p.55)

»→ **Salsa Verde** (see p.55)

»→ **Roasted Garlic Crema** (see p.59)

PORK PIBIL

SERVES 4

This parcel will blow your mind. Whatever that achiote is doing to the pork, it sure as hell works! This recipe takes a bit of time, and those banana leaves, although readily available online, are not a supermarket staple. Consider this dish a Mexican replacement for a Sunday roast. You'll want to eat it every week.

YOU WILL NEED

1.3kg pork belly, skin and three-quarters of the fat removed

4 banana leaves or large sheets of baking paper

3 tomatoes, charred (see p.26) and sliced

1 large green pepper, charred (see p.26) and sliced

1 large onion, sliced and charred (see p.26)

3 bay leaves

4 warmed tortillas

FOR THE MARINADE

2 dried chipotle meco chillies

15g lard

25g achiote paste

1 teaspoon dried oregano, preferably Mexican

¼ teaspoon ground cloves

2.5cm piece of cinnamon stick, crumbled

½ teaspoon black peppercorns

1 teaspoon cumin seeds

1 teaspoon ground allspice

3 garlic cloves, dry roasted (see p.26)

2 tablespoons orange juice

2 tablespoons lemon juice

2 tablespoons lime juice

2 tablespoons white wine vinegar

1 tablespoon chipotles en adobo

1 teaspoon sea salt, plus extra for seasoning

First, make the marinade. Using tongs, hold the meco chillies over a hob for 1 minute, or until starting to darken. Place in a heatproof bowl and cover with just-boiled water. Press the chillies down to submerge, then leave to soak for 20 minutes, until softened. Drain and remove the stems and seeds. Discard the soaking water.

Meanwhile, heat the lard in a large frying pan over a medium heat, crumble in the achiote paste and add the oregano, cloves, cinnamon, peppercorns, cumin and allspice and cook, stirring, until it smells aromatic, about 1–2 minutes. Tip into a food processor with the rest of the marinade ingredients (including the rehydrated chillies) and blend until smooth.

Put the pork belly in a non-metallic dish, stab the top with a skewer, then spoon the marinade all over, rubbing it into the holes. Cover and leave to marinate in the fridge for 8 hours, or overnight if you have time – the longer, the better.

Preheat the oven to 170°C/325°F/Gas 3.

Arrange the banana leaves or sheets of baking paper so that they overlap in a roasting tin. Arrange the tomatoes, green pepper, onion and bay leaves in the middle to create a bed for the pork belly. Place the pork belly and any marinade left in the dish on top of the vegetables and fold the sides and then the ends of the banana leaves or baking paper over to make a parcel. Secure with kitchen string. Roast for 2–3 hours, until the pork is very tender, then open the parcel and tear the meat into chunks. Serve in the opened parcel for everyone to make their own burritos, adding some of the vegetables and juices, along with the fillings (below).

FILL YOUR BURRITOS

To complete your burritos, use 1 recipe quantity of:

»→ **Coriander & Lime Rice** (see p.37)

»→ **Smoky Corn Salsa** (see p.50)

»→ **Tomatillo & Avocado Salsa** (see p.54)

»→ **Crema de Comal** (see p.59)

PULLED PORK TAMALES

SERVES 6

If you haven't yet had a tamale now's your chance. The Mexican equivalent of Cornish pasties, tamales are sold by street vendors across Mexico with fillings from cheese to chilli to... steak and ale (okay, maybe not that one – for Book Two?). We've stuffed these tasty guys with some shredded pork and paired them up with a delicious salsa.

YOU WILL NEED

6 dried corn husks

425g pulled pork from the Pork Carnitas (see p.123), at room temperature

FOR THE TAMALE MASA

90g lard, softened

1 teaspoon sea salt

1 teaspoon baking powder

270g fine cornmeal or polenta

300ml double-strength beef stock

FOR THE TAMALE SAUCE

3–5 large dried ancho chillies, to taste

2 tablespoons lime juice

½ onion, sliced and charred (see p.26)

1 teaspoon sea salt

3 garlic cloves, dry roasted (see p.26)

210g fresh tomatillos, charred (see p.26) and chopped; or use 210g tinned tomatillos, well drained and chopped

Put the dried corn husks in a large bowl and pour enough just-boiled water over to cover. Leave to soak for 15 minutes, until softened, then drain well and pat dry.

Meanwhile, make the tamale masa. Cream the lard with an electric mixer or wooden spoon for about 5 minutes, until light and fluffy. Beat in the salt and baking powder. Gradually add the cornmeal and stock, alternating between the two and occasionally scraping down the sides of the bowl, until you have a soft paste, a bit like wet hummus. Spoon into a container and chill, uncovered (the mixture needs to breathe), until ready to use.

To make the sauce, put the ancho chillies in a saucepan, cover with just-boiled water and soak for 10 minutes, until softened. Drain, reserving 3 tablespoons of the soaking water, then remove the stems and seeds. Put the soaked chillies in a blender with the rest of the sauce ingredients and saved soaking water and blend until smooth. Spoon the sauce into a bowl and stir in the pork until combined.

To assemble the tamales, place about 2 tablespoons of the masa dough, depending on the size of your corn husks, in the centre of an opened-out husk. Spread into a rectangle, about 3mm thick and leaving a 1cm border. Put 2 heaped tablespoons of the pork mixture on top and fold one side of the husk over the filling, followed by the opposite side. Fold over one end to cover the seam and tie a thin strip of corn husk (or kitchen string) around to hold the tamale together and make a parcel. Repeat to make 6 tamales.

Lay the tamales in a steamer basket, it doesn't matter if they overlap and are in layers. Steam for 1 hour, replenishing the water when necessary. Arrange on a serving plate and serve straightaway.

OPPOSITE: **PORK PIBIL (P.126)**
THIS PAGE: **PULLED PORK TAMALES (P.127)**

NOAH'S ARK

When Noah filled the ark with animals, we bet he didn't think that one day the ark would be a burrito to blow your mind (and your belly). Start with a bed of shredded cos lettuce leaves, then fill up this bad boy with meat from the following: Chilango Chicken (p.74), Steak Fajitas (p.103), Camarón Rojo (p.138) and Porchetta (p.124). Then, top with Smoky Corn Salsa (p.50) and Chipotle Crema (p.58). To finish, sprinkle with a little coriander and sliced red jalapeño chilli.

FISH & SEAFOOD

MEXICO HAS THE ATLANTIC ON ONE SIDE AND THE PACIFIC ON THE OTHER. THAT'S A LOT OF OCEAN. HELL! THE BAJA CALIFORNIA PENINSULA IS SUR-ROUNDED BY WATER (AS A SIDE NOTE, IT WOULD TAKE YOU 18 HOURS TO DRIVE FROM THE SOUTHERN TIP OF THE PENINSULA TO THE US BORDER – THAT'S A LONG STRIP OF LAND). THE SEA IS PART OF MEXICO, SO IT MAKES SENSE TO INCLUDE SOME TASTY FISH RECIPES IN A BOOK ABOUT (MOSTLY) MEXICAN FOOD.

HOWEVER, THROWING SEAFOOD INSIDE A BURRITO ISN'T AN EASY TASK. THE DENSITY OF THE VARIOUS INGREDIENTS EASILY DROWNS OUT THE DELICATE TEXTURE AND FLAVOURS OF FISH. SO, IN THIS SECTION WE'RE SWITCHING THINGS UP WITH SOME TACOS, AS WELL AS SOME BURRITOS, TO LET THOSE FISHES SING.

MACKEREL ESCABECHE

This burrito is going to mess with your head a little. The dish is effectively fish 'cooked' in acid – not like dropping acid in the 90s, but the vinegar type. It's a warm summer's day picnic burrito – the fish is served cold.

YOU WILL NEED

4 large mackerel fillets, pin-boned

4 warmed tortillas

FOR THE PICKLING LIQUOR

230ml white wine vinegar

½ teaspoon whole black peppercorns

1½ teaspoons coriander seeds

1 bay leaf

1½ teaspoons whole allspice berries

2.5cm piece of cinnamon stick

2 garlic cloves, thinly sliced

1 thyme sprig

100g granulated sugar

½ teaspoon sea salt

coriander leaves

FOR THE PICKLED VEGETABLES

1 tablespoon vegetable oil, plus extra for cooking the fish

½ red onion, very thinly sliced

1 carrot, cut into julienne strips

½ red pepper, deseeded and cut into julienne strips

½ yellow pepper, deseeded and cut into julienne strips

1 green jalapeño chilli, charred (see p.26) and thinly sliced

Put the ingredients for the pickling liquor with 350ml of water in a saucepan and bring almost to the boil. Reduce the heat and simmer for 30 minutes, until reduced by about half. Strain the pickling liquor and discard the aromatics.

Meanwhile, make the pickled vegetables. Heat the vegetable oil in a large frying pan over a medium heat. Add the onion, turn the heat down to low and gently sauté for 3 minutes, stirring often. Add the remaining vegetables and sauté for another 2 minutes – they should still have a bit of crunch. Transfer the vegetables to a bowl and add the jalapeño. Pour a quarter of the pickling liquor over and turn until combined.

Return the remaining pickling liquor to the pan and let it simmer while you prepare the fish. Wipe the frying pan clean, add enough oil to coat the bottom of the pan and heat over a medium–high heat. Place the mackerel in the pan, skin-side down, and cook for 2 minutes, holding the fillets down with a spatula for the first 45 seconds to prevent them curling.

Place the mackerel in a non-metallic dish and pour the pickling liquor over. Leave to cool, then cover and marinate in the fridge for 3 hours. Break up each fillet over 1 warmed tortilla. Fill as below, top with the pickled vegetables, sprinkle with coriander leaves to taste, then roll.

WHY NOT...

Try swapping the mackerel with another type of fish, such as small fillets of sea bass or herring. The fish just needs to be thin enough to allow the hot pickling liquid to penetrate and preserve it.

FILL YOUR BURRITOS

To complete your burritos, use 1 recipe quantity of:

»→ **Coriander & Lime Rice** (see p.37)

»→ **Tomatillo & Avocado Salsa** (see p.54)

SERVES 4

PRAWNS WITH CHORIZO

This one is kinda what it says on the tin. Delicious in a burrito as it is here, it's also amazing in a taco. The Roasted Garlic Crema on page 59 turns this recipe from great to godly.

YOU WILL NEED

250g cooking chorizo, peeled and sliced into 5mm-thick rounds

vegetable oil, for frying

350g large, raw tiger prawns, peeled and deveined

1 red habanero chilli, charred (see p.26), deseeded and finely chopped

2 garlic cloves, crushed

1 large ripe Hass avocado, halved, stoned, and flesh cut into 1cm chunks

sea salt and ground black pepper

4 warmed tortillas

1 lime, for squeezing

Arrange the chorizo in a large, cold frying pan and then place over a medium heat. Gently cook the chorizo for 8 minutes, turning once, to allow the oil to render out. Remove the chorizo with a slotted spoon, leaving the oil in the pan.

Continue heating the oil over a medium heat, adding a splash of vegetable oil if there isn't enough from the chorizo to coat the base of the pan. Toss the prawns in the chilli and garlic and add to the pan. Fry for about 2 minutes on each side, or until cooked and golden. Return the chorizo to the pan and turn until combined. Season with salt and pepper to taste, bearing in mind that the chorizo is quite salty. Divide into 4 equal portions, and use each portion to top a warmed tortilla. Scatter over the avocado, fill as below, squeeze over some lime, then roll.

FILL YOUR BURRITOS

To complete your burritos, use 1 recipe quantity of:

»→ Coriander & Lime Rice (see p.37)

»→ Pico de Gallo (see p.55)

»→ Roasted Garlic Crema (see p.59)

CLOCKWISE FROM ABOVE: **MACKEREL ESCABECHE (P.134),
PRAWNS WITH CHORIZO (P.135), CAMARÓN ROJO (P.138)**

CAMARÓN ROJO

The marinade for these prawns also makes a divine salsa rojo, which is amazing cooked or uncooked. Camarón is simply prawn, by the way. And, as with most things in life, the bigger the better. Per burrito you should allow for about 8–10 decent-sized prawns; for a taco you could half that. And please, cook them through safely but, whatever you do, do not *overcook* them.

YOU WILL NEED

400g large tiger prawns, peeled
   and deveined
4 warmed tortillas
coriander leaves
slices of red jalapeño chilli

FOR THE MARINADE

1 large dried chipotle meco chilli
½ teaspoon cumin seeds
1 tomato, charred (see p.26) and finely
   chopped
1 large garlic clove, crushed
juice and finely grated zest of ½ lime
2 red jalapeño chillies
1 tablespoon vegetable oil, plus extra
   for cooking
sea salt and ground black pepper

To make the marinade, put the meco chilli in a heatproof bowl and pour over enough just-boiled water to cover. Press the chilli down to submerge, then leave to soak for 20 minutes, until softened. Drain the chilli, then remove the stem and seeds and roughly chop. Discard the soaking water.

Toast the cumin seeds in a dry frying pan for about 1 minute, or until they smell aromatic, then tip into a mortar and grind with the pestle to a powder. Put the cumin, soaked meco and other marinade ingredients in a mini food processor or blender and blend until smooth. Season with salt and pepper, to taste.

Put the prawns in a non-metallic dish and spoon the marinade over until the prawns are coated. Cover and leave to marinate in the fridge for 1 hour.

Heat a large griddle pan over a medium–high heat. When hot, brush with oil and carefully add the prawns (you will probably need to cook them in 2 batches). Griddle the prawns for 2 minutes on each side, or until pink and cooked through. Divide the prawns into 4 equal portions, using each portion to top a warmed tortilla. Fill as below, sprinkle with coriander leaves and chilli slices to taste, then roll.

FILL YOUR BURRITOS

To complete your burritos, use 1 recipe quantity of:

»→ **Pico de Gallo** (see p.55)
»→ **Red Taquería Salsa** (see p.54)
»→ **Baja Cabbage Slaw** (see p.64)

BAJA FISH TACOS

One of my favourite trips to Mexico was down the Baja peninsula to Los Cabos. This red snapper dusted in seasoned flour makes for a wonderful taco that is perfectly completed with our Roasted Pineapple Salsa (see p.50).

YOU WILL NEED

1 tomato, charred (see p.26), deseeded and roughly chopped

15g achiote paste

juice of 1 lime, plus wedges to serve

2 teaspoons vegetable oil

2 teaspoons agave syrup or nectar

25g chipotles en adobo, chopped

4 red snapper fillets, rinsed and patted dry, each fillet cut into quarters to make 4 long pieces

200g plain flour

1 teaspoon sea salt, plus extra for seasoning

½ teaspoon ground black pepper, plus extra for seasoning

vegetable oil, for deep frying

8–12 warmed small tortillas

Put the tomato, achiote paste, lime juice, oil, agave and chipotles en adobo in a blender and blitz to a purée. Season with the salt and pepper.

Put the red snapper in a shallow dish and spoon over the tomato marinade. Cover and marinate in the fridge for 30 minutes.

Pour enough oil into a large, deep saucepan or deep-fat fryer to deep-fry the fish. Heat the oil to 185°C/365°F, or until a cube of day-old bread turns crisp and golden in 45 seconds. Turn on the oven to low.

Put the flour in a separate dish and season with the salt and pepper. Remove 4 snapper pieces from the marinade, dunk into the seasoned flour and shake off any excess. Place in the hot oil and deep-fry for 5 minutes, until crisp and golden brown. Scoop out the fish with a slotted spoon and set aside to drain on kitchen paper. Repeat with the remaining fish pieces, keeping the cooked and drained fish warm in the oven. Divide the fish pieces into 8–12 equal portions, using each portion to top a warmed taco. Fill as below, then serve open with lime wedges for squeezing over.

FILL YOUR TACOS

To complete your tacos, use 1 recipe quantity of:

»→ Baja Cabbage Slaw (see p.64)

»→ Roasted Pineapple Salsa (see p.50)

»→ Chipotle Crema (see p.58)

OPPOSITE: **BAJA FISH TACOS (P.139)** THIS PAGE (TOP): **CHIPOTLE SALMON TACOS (P.142)** THIS PAGE (BOTTOM, LEFT AND RIGHT): **LOBSTER IN BASIL & CHIPOTLE BUTTER TACOS (P.143)**

SERVES 4

CHIPOTLE SALMON TACOS

Mexican cuisine is about making the best of inexpensive ingredients, but salmon doesn't count. Go to a fishmonger or the fish counter in the supermarket and spend a little extra. This recipe won't work with frozen or tinned salmon – it has to be fresh. We recommend the Roasted Pineapple Salsa on page 50 with these tacos, but they will also taste delicious with the Chipotle Crema on page 58.

YOU WILL NEED

400g salmon fillets, about
   2 large
8–12 warmed small tortillas
2 limes, cut into wedges
chopped coriander leaves

FOR THE MARINADE

½ teaspoon chipotle powder
finely grated zest of 1 lime
4 tablespoons olive oil
¼ teaspoon fine sea salt
ground black pepper, to taste

Using a sharp knife, make light diagonal cuts in the skin of each salmon fillet and place the fillets in a non-metallic dish. Mix together the ingredients for the marinade and spoon it over the salmon until coated. Cover and leave to marinate in the fridge for 1 hour.

Preheat the oven to 180°C/350°F/Gas 4.

Heat a large, ridged griddle pan over a high heat. Add the salmon, skin-side down, and use a spatula to hold the fish flat for 30 seconds, then reduce the heat to medium. After 2 minutes, turn the fish over and cook for a further 2 minutes.

Transfer the salmon to an ovenproof dish and place in the oven for 3–5 minutes, or until just opaque in the middle. Roughly flake the salmon, discarding the skin. Divide the salmon into 8–12 equal portions, using each portion to top a warmed tortilla. Fill as below, sprinkle with chopped coriander and serve open with wedges of lime for squeezing over.

FILL YOUR TACOS

To complete your tacos, use 1 recipe quantity of:
- → **Roasted Pineapple Salsa (see p.50)**
- → **Charred Pineapple with Quick Pickled Jalapeños (see p.153)**
- → **Charred Jalapeño Guacamole (see p.56)**

LOBSTER IN BASIL & CHIPOTLE BUTTER TACOS

Indulgence, indulgence, indulgence – what's not to like about a bit of lobster in a taco? You can even throw in some steak, if you like: Surf 'n' Turf tacos, right there.

YOU WILL NEED

4 x 85–115g uncooked lobster tails, defrosted
8 warmed small tortillas

FOR THE BASIL & CHIPOTLE BUTTER

250g unsalted butter, softened to room temperature
1 handful of basil leaves, thinly sliced
1 garlic clove, crushed
1 teaspoon chipotle powder
finely grated zest of 1 lime
1 teaspoon sea salt
ground black pepper, to taste

Using a wooden spoon, beat together all the ingredients for the basil and chipotle butter until evenly combined.

Place 2 layers of cling film on a worktop. Spoon the butter in a line across the middle and roll into a roulade. Twist each end of the cling film to make a sausage shape, then chill the flavoured butter until needed.

Bring a large saucepan of water to the boil. Insert a skewer into each lobster tail to keep it straight while cooking. Place the tails, 2 at a time, in the boiling water and cook over a rolling boil, covered, for 4–6 minutes, or until cooked through. Using tongs, remove the cooked lobster from the pan and refresh in a bowl of iced water. Repeat with the remaining lobster tails. Remove the skewers, peel the tails and pat dry with kitchen paper.

Heat a large, ridged griddle pan or chargrill over a high heat until smoking.

Cut the lobster tails in half lengthways and place, cut-side down in the hot griddle pan for 1 minute.

Melt the flavoured butter in a large frying pan over a medium heat, add the lobster tails and continue to spoon the butter over until it becomes nutty and brown, about 2 minutes. Top each warmed tortilla with some Pico de Gallo (see below) and finish with a lobster tail. Serve straightaway.

FILL YOUR TACOS

To complete your tacos, use 1 recipe quantity of:
→ Pico de Gallo (see p.55)

TACO PLATTER

We think our recipes are so good it's hard to share, but Mexicans love a party (don't we all). Tacos make for superb party food. Lay out the warmed small tortillas, lay out the fillings – Baja Fish Tacos (p.139), Camarón Rojo (p.138), Prawns with Chorizo (p.135), Mackerel Escabeche (p.134) and Chipotle Salmon Tacos (p.142) – and serve with Hot Mexican Quinoa (p.42) and Baja Cabbage Slaw (p.64), and salsas and cremas of your choice (see pp.50–59). Then, let everyone dig in to build their own tacos. Oh, and don't forget the margaritas – although it could get messy (in more ways than one).

VEGGIE

THE FLAVOUR AND SPICE PALATE OF MEXICAN CUISINE IS TRULY EXTRAORDINARY. WHICH MEANS YOU CAN SAY A FOND FAREWELL TO THE DAYS OF BLAND-TASTING VEGGIE MEALS. WE'VE GOT YOUR TASTE BUDS COVERED WITH A SPECIAL LITTLE RANGE OF FLAVOUR BOMBS, FROM PULLED OYSTER MUSHROOMS AND ACHIOTE BAKED AUBERGINES TO SOME DELICIOUS BEAN AND QUINOA OPTIONS. OH, AND YOU JUST HAVE TO TRY THE CHILLI NON CARNE (THANKS DANNY).

PULLED OYSTER MUSHROOMS

SERVES 4

When we first made these mushroom burritos, the filling looked so like shredded chicken, we had to take a second look.

YOU WILL NEED

500g oyster mushrooms, wiped
   and stalks trimmed
4 warmed tortillas

FOR THE SAUCE

3 tablespoons agave syrup or nectar
80g chipotles en adobo, finely
   chopped
100ml orange juice
50ml lime juice
2 garlic cloves, crushed
1 bay leaf
2 teaspoons ground cumin
1½ tablespoons vegetable oil,
   plus extra for greasing
1 teaspoon sea salt

To make the sauce, mix together half the agave with the rest of the ingredients and 150ml of water in a large sauté pan with a lid. Then, add the mushrooms and carefully turn them in the sauce, until coated. Bring to the boil, then reduce the heat to low and simmer, covered, for 30–35 minutes, until the mushrooms are very tender and the sauce has evaporated. Leave to cool for 5 minutes.

Meanwhile, preheat the oven to 180°C/350°F/Gas 4. Lightly grease 2 baking trays.

Shred the mushrooms into strips. Spread the strips onto the prepared trays in an even layer. Drizzle the remaining agave over the top and roast for 17–20 minutes, until the edges of the mushrooms turn golden and start to crisp. Divide the mushroom into 4 equal portions, using one portion to top each warmed tortilla. Fill as below, then roll.

FILL YOUR BURRITOS

To complete your burritos, use 1 recipe quantity of:
»→ **Coriander & Lime Rice** (see p.37)
»→ **Chipotle Black Beans** (see p.47)
»→ **Roasted Habanero Salsa** (see p.51)
»→ **Crema de Comal** (see p.59)

ACHIOTE BAKED AUBERGINES

Candy pecans are the highlight in this recipe, and together with the incredible cream sauce, they turn this baked aubergine dish almost into a dessert.

YOU WILL NEED

2 large aubergines

10g chipotles en adobo

20g achiote paste, crumbled

4 teaspoons vegetable oil, plus extra for drizzling

50g pecan nuts

2 teaspoons agave syrup or nectar

thick plain yogurt, to serve

4 warmed tortillas

FOR THE ANCHO & CACAO SALT

1 tablespoon raw cacao powder

1 tablespoon ancho chilli powder

¼ teaspoon chipotle powder

¼ teaspoon ground black pepper

1 teaspoon sea salt

1½ tablespoons caster sugar

Preheat the grill to its highest setting. Place the aubergines on a grill pan and char under the grill for about 20–25 minutes, turning them occasionally, until the skin darkens and starts to crisp and the flesh becomes tender. Alternatively, char the aubergines over a gas hob, or use a blow torch (see p.26).

Place the charred aubergines in a bowl, cover with cling film and leave for 30 minutes to loosen the skins. Gently remove all the skin, keeping the aubergines whole.

Meanwhile, preheat the oven to 180°C/350°F/Gas 4. Blend the chipotles en adobo with the achiote paste and 2 tablespoons of water until smooth. Mix together all the ingredients for the ancho and cacao salt.

Place the aubergines in a roasting tin. Brush the achiote marinade generously all over and sprinkle a tablespoon of the ancho and cacao salt over the top of each one. Drizzle over the oil and roast for 20 minutes, until golden and tender.

Fifteen minutes before the aubergines are ready, toss the pecans in the agave syrup and add a generous sprinkling of the ancho and cacao salt. Spread out evenly on a baking tray and bake for 5 minutes, until sticky and golden, then leave to cool and roughly chop.

Serve the aubergines whole with the yogurt and pecans (dusted with a little extra ancho and cacao salt) on the side, along with the burrito fillings (below). Give everyone a warmed tortilla and allow them to help themselves.

FILL YOUR BURRITOS

To complete your burritos, use 1 recipe quantity of:

→ **Coriander & Lime Rice** (see p.37)

→ **Chipotle Black Beans** (see p.47)

→ **Tomatillo & Avocado Salsa** (see p.54)

VEGGIE **149**

CLOCKWISE FROM TOP LEFT: **PULLED OYSTER MUSHROOMS (P.148), ACHIOTE BAKED AUBERGINES (P.149), CHARRED PINEAPPLE WITH QUICK PICKLED JALAPEÑOS (P.153), CHILLI NON-CARNE (P.152)**

CHILLI NON-CARNE

We launched this dish on the menu in May 2017 and it became an instant hit. It's a nice stew for a bowl with rice, and a little messy for a burrito. It's also tasty with a topper of steak if you're not actually vegetarian.

YOU WILL NEED

600g sweet potatoes, peeled and cut into bite-sized chunks

3 tablespoons olive oil

1 teaspoon sea salt

½ teaspoon ground black pepper

400g tomatoes, charred (see p.26)

3 onions, finely chopped

2 garlic cloves, crushed

1 small red pepper, deseeded and chopped

1 small green pepper, deseeded and chopped

3 tablespoons tomato purée

2 teaspoons smoked paprika

1 teaspoon ground coriander

1 teaspoon cumin seeds

½ teaspoon ground star anise

½ teaspoon ground cinnamon

1 teaspoon chipotle powder

2 x 400g tins of kidney beans, drained and rinsed

800ml vegetable stock

80ml BBQ Sauce (see p.91), or use ready-made

1 teaspoon liquid smoke

2 teaspoons dark brown soft sugar

1 large handful of coriander leaves, chopped

Arroz Verde (see p.40), to serve

Preheat the oven to 180°C/350°F/Gas 4. Put the sweet potatoes in a large bowl, add a third of the oil and season with some of the salt and pepper, then turn until combined. Tip onto a baking tray, spread out evenly and roast for 30 minutes, turning halfway through, or until tender and starting to colour.

Meanwhile, put the tomatoes in a food processor and blend to a coarse purée. Set aside.

Heat the remaining oil in a large heavy-based saucepan over a medium heat. Add the onions and fry for 10 minutes, stirring occasionally, until softened. Add the garlic, all the peppers, the tomato purée, the salt and all the spices and cook for 5 minutes, stirring.

Add the blended tomatoes, kidney beans, stock, barbecue sauce, liquid smoke, seasoning and sugar and bring up to the boil, then reduce the heat to low and simmer for 30 minutes, part-covered, stirring occasionally.

Stir in the sweet potatoes and cook, part-covered, for another 15–20 minutes, until the sauce has reduced and thickened. (If the sauce is too runny during cooking, remove the lid entirely; alternatively cover completely to stop the chilli drying out.) Stir in the coriander, then serve with the cooked Arroz Verde.

CHARRED PINEAPPLE WITH QUICK PICKLED JALAPEÑOS

A delicious and fresh vegan taco with a touch of spice. But beware, as light as they seem, these tacos can easily tempt you to stuff yourself to oblivion.

YOU WILL NEED

1 small pineapple, about 450g, cut into 1cm-thick slices and charred (see p.26), core removed and cut into bite-sized chunks

1 red pepper, deseeded and cut into bite-sized chunks

½ bunch of spring onions, thinly sliced

1 green jalapeño chilli, charred (see p.26), deseeded and diced

8–12 warmed tacos

coriander leaves

FOR THE QUICK PICKLED JALAPEÑOS

150ml raw, unfiltered apple cider vinegar

2½ tablespoons caster sugar

1 teaspoon sea salt

1 teaspoon coriander seeds

1 bay leaf

5 red jalapeño chillies, deseeded and thinly sliced into rounds

FOR THE DRESSING

4 tablespoons pineapple juice

1 tablespoon light soy sauce

1 tablespoon light brown soft sugar

1cm piece of root ginger, peeled and finely chopped

1 garlic clove, crushed

First make the pickled jalapeños. Put the vinegar, sugar, salt, coriander seeds and bay leaf in a saucepan with 3 tablespoons of water. Bring to the boil, stirring until the sugar dissolves, then reduce the heat and simmer for 3 minutes. Put the chillies in a shallow bowl and pour over the pickling liquid. Set aside for 2 hours to let the pickle infuse the chillies.

To make the dressing, put all the ingredients in a small saucepan and simmer for 1 minute, stirring until the sugar dissolves. Pour the dressing into a bowl and leave to cool.

Mix the pineapple with the red pepper, spring onions and charred jalapeño. Spoon over the dressing and add a few slices of the pickled chilli. Any leftover pickle will keep for up to 1 month stored in an airtight container in the fridge. Divide the pineapple mixture into 8–12 equal portions and use each portion to top a warmed taco. Fill as below, sprinkle with coriander leaves, then serve. Alternatively, place the tacos and all the fillings on the table for everyone to help themselves.

FILL YOUR TACOS

To complete your tacos, use 1 recipe quantity of:

»→ Hot Mexican Quinoa (see p.42)

»→ Smoky Corn Salsa (see p.50)

»→ Lime & Jalapeño Crema (see p.58)

»→ Pickled Onions (see p.50)

NACHO MOUNTAIN

What better for a party than mountains of shop-bought tortilla chips, laden with gooèy Monterey Jack and Cheddar cheeses, then toasted in the oven and topped with Mexican deliciousness before serving. Start with Chipotle Black Beans (p.47), both guacs (p.56) and go on to offer Pico de Gallo (p.55), Smoky Tomato Salsa (p.51) and Chipotle Crema (p.58), along with some slices of red jalapeño. For your non-veggie friends, provide some Chilango Fried Chicken (p.82) and pulled pork (p.122) alongside, if you like.

MEXICAN BBQ PULLED CELERIAC

This gnarly barbecue delight came to us after we tried to make some pancakes with celeriac and we're like, "Let's just shred it... oh, hang on... that works. Pass me the barbecue sauce." Eureka! As Archimedes would've said.

YOU WILL NEED

1 celeriac (about 600g), peeled and quartered
2 tablespoons olive oil
1 teaspoon sea salt
½ recipe quantity of BBQ Sauce (see p.91)
4 warmed tortillas

Preheat the oven to 180°C/350°F/Gas 4.

Put the celeriac in an ovenproof dish and toss it in the oil and salt until coated. Cover the dish with foil and roast the celeriac for 1½ hours, turning halfway through cooking, until light golden and very tender when pierced with a skewer.

Remove from the oven and shred or "pull" the celeriac using 2 forks. Place the celeriac on a lined baking tray and spoon over half the barbecue sauce, then turn until thoroughly coated. Return to the oven for 20 minutes, or until the edges of the celeriac start to crisp up and turn deep golden. Slather in more barbecue sauce, then divide into 4 equal portions, using each portion to top a warmed tortilla. Fill as below, then roll.

FILL YOUR BURRITOS

To complete your burritos, use 1 recipe quantity of:
»→ **Baja Cabbage Slaw** (see p.64)
»→ **Classic Guacamole** (see p.56)

MEXICAN ROASTED VEGETABLES WITH TEQUILA BEANS

These beans have a kick of tequila that will remind you of your clubbing days. However, you're also honouring your body with goodness in the lightly roasted root veg and shallots (and more), and charred jalapeño. And there's no hangover.

YOU WILL NEED

4 tablespoons olive oil

1 teaspoon sea salt

1 teaspoon smoked paprika

½ teaspoon chipotle powder

½ teaspoon ground cumin

1 green jalapeño chilli, finely chopped

500g pumpkin or butternut squash, deseeded and flesh cut into bite-sized chunks

2 sweet potatoes, peeled and cut into bite-sized chunks

2 carrots, preferably 1 yellow and 1 purple, cut into chunks

4 banana shallots, peeled but left whole

1 large red pepper, deseeded and cut into large pieces

2 courgettes, halved lengthways and thickly sliced

4 garlic cloves, left whole

80g goat's cheese, crumbled

1 handful of pumpkin seeds

1 handful of coriander leaves, chopped

Hot Mexican Quinoa (see p.42), to serve

FOR THE TEQUILA BEANS

1 tablespoon olive oil

1 shallot, thinly sliced

1 garlic clove, crushed

½ teaspoon ground cumin

1 teaspoon sea salt

4 tablespoons of tequila

400g tin of pinto beans, drained and rinsed

juice of 1 lime

1 handful of coriander leaves, chopped

Preheat the oven to 180°C/350°F/Gas 4.

Mix together the oil, salt, smoked paprika, chipotle powder, cumin and jalapeño in a bowl. Put the pumpkin or squash, sweet potatoes, carrots and shallots in a large bowl, pour over three-quarters of the spice oil and toss until the vegetables are coated in the oil mixture. Tip the vegetables onto a large baking tray and spread out into an even layer.

Put the red pepper, courgettes and garlic cloves in the large bowl, pour over the remaining spice oil, turn until coated, then tip onto a separate large baking tray and spread out evenly. Roast the root vegetables for 40 minutes, turning once, until tender and starting to colour. Roast the second tray of vegetables and garlic for 20–25 minutes, until tender and starting to colour.

While the vegetables are roasting, make the tequila beans. Heat the oil in a pan over a medium heat. Add the shallot and garlic and fry for 5 minutes, until softened. Stir in the cumin, salt and tequila and simmer until the tequila has reduced by half. Stir in the pinto beans, lime juice and coriander, heat through briefly and remove from the heat. Squeeze the roasted garlic out of its skin into the beans and turn until combined.

To serve, spoon the roasted vegetables onto a large serving plate and scatter over the crumbled goat's cheese, pumpkin seeds and coriander leaves. Serve with the tequila beans and Hot Mexican Quinoa.

CLOCKWISE FROM TOP LEFT: **MEXICAN BBQ PULLED CELERIAC (P.156), MEXICAN ROASTED VEGETABLES WITH TEQUILA BEANS (P.157), GRANJERO ESTAFADO (P.160)**

GRANJERO ESTAFADO

I love pumpkin. Growing up I used always to look forward to my Ma's pumpkin pies on Thanksgiving. Now, this isn't a pumpkin pie, of course. And it's not even a dessert. It's a farmer's stew where the humble pumpkin features nice and strong.

YOU WILL NEED

600g pumpkin or butternut squash, deseeded and flesh cut into bite-sized chunks

3 tablespoons vegetable oil

15g dried ancho chillies

1 large onion, sliced and charred (see p.26)

4 garlic cloves, thinly sliced

1 teaspoon cumin seeds

20g achiote paste

2 teaspoons smoked paprika

1 large sweet potato, about 300g, peeled and cut into bite-sized chunks

30g chipotles en adobo

1 large bunch of coriander, leaves and stalks separated, stalks roughly chopped

1 teaspoon sea salt

2 teaspoons dried oregano, preferably Mexican

1 bay leaf

800ml vegetable stock

400g tin of pinto beans, drained and rinsed

juice of 1 lime

Coriander & Lime Rice (see p.37), to serve

Smoky Corn Salsa (see p.50), to serve

Preheat the oven to 200°C/400°F/Gas 6.

Toss the pumpkin or squash in 1 tablespoon of the oil, place it on a baking tray and roast for 25 minutes, turning once, until soft and starting to turn golden.

Meanwhile, using tongs, hold the ancho chillies over the flame of a hob for a minute or so, until toasted (or do this in a large dry frying pan, turning once, until they start to smell toasted). Place in a heatproof bowl and cover with just-boiled water. Press the chillies down so they are submerged, then leave to soak for 20 minutes, until softened. Remove the stems and seeds and finely chop. Discard the soaking water.

Heat the remaining oil in a large heavy-based casserole over a medium heat. Add the onion and fry for 8 minutes, until softened. Turn down the heat slightly and add the garlic, cumin seeds, achiote paste and smoked paprika and cook, stirring to break up the paste, for 1 minute.

Next, add the sweet potato, chopped ancho chillies, chipotles en adobo, coriander stalks, salt, oregano, bay leaf and stock and bring to the boil. Reduce the heat and simmer, part-covered with a lid, for 40 minutes, stirring occasionally.

Add the pinto beans and roasted pumpkin or squash and cook for another 20 minutes, until the sauce has reduced by half and thickened. Stir in the lime juice and coriander leaves, and serve with the Coriander & Lime Rice and Smoky Corn Salsa.

ROASTED SQUASH QUINOA BOWL

SERVES 4

As I've said before: I love a pumpkin. And I'm not about to stop. For a non-veggie tip, the chipotle-spiced butternut squash makes for a delicious base that goes beautifully with either the chicken or beef fajitas.

YOU WILL NEED

3 tablespoons chipotles en adobo

1½ tablespoons vegetable oil

½ teaspoon sea salt, plus extra to taste

¼ teaspoon ground black pepper, plus extra to taste

400g butternut squash, peeled, deseeded and flesh cut into bite-sized chunks

350g quinoa

200g pineapple, peeled and sliced into rounds, then charred (see p.26)

4 tomatoes, charred (see p.26) and finely chopped

40g baby spinach leaves, chopped

juice of 1 lime

1 handful of chopped coriander leaves

2 corn on the cobs, charred (see p.26), kernels stripped

your choice of crema (see pp.58–9), to serve

Preheat the oven to 180°C/350°F/Gas 4.

Put the chipotles en adobo, oil, salt and pepper in a mini food processor or blender and blend to a paste. Put the butternut squash in a mixing bowl and stir in the chipotle paste until coated. Tip the squash onto a baking tray and spread out evenly. Roast for 30–35 minutes, turning once, until tender and golden.

Meanwhile, cook the quinoa according to the packet instructions. Drain, if necessary, then season to taste and fluff up with a fork.

Core and dice the charred pineapple and put it in a serving bowl with the cooked quinoa and roasted squash, and the tomatoes and spinach. Season to taste and fold in the lime juice and coriander. Scatter the corn kernels over and drizzle with your choice of crema before serving.

CENTRE (TOP): **ROASTED SQUASH QUINOA BOWL (P.161)**
OPPOSITE (BOTTOM): **SMOKY BEAN BOWL (P.164)**
THIS PAGE (BELOW AND BOTTOM): **SPICY PEPPER, BROCCOLI
& AVOCADO RICE BOWL (P.165)**

SMOKY BEAN BOWL

This tastes off-the-scale amazing. Frankly, there's nothing more to say on the matter. If you don't want it as a meal in itself, you must provide it as an accompaniment at a barbecue, or at a throwback 70s-style buffet.

YOU WILL NEED

400g tin of black beans, drained and
  rinsed

400g tin of red kidney beans, drained
  and rinsed

30g chipotles en adobo, finely
  chopped

1 small red onion, sliced, charred
  (see p.26) and chopped

2 corn on the cobs, charred (see p.26),
  kernels stripped

1 good handful of coriander leaves,
  chopped

1 red jalapeño chilli, deseeded and
  thinly sliced

FOR THE DRESSING

juice of 2 limes

3 tablespoons extra-virgin olive oil

½ teaspoon sea salt

¼ teaspoon ground black pepper

Mix together all the ingredients for the dressing until combined. Set aside.

Mix together the beans with the chipotles en adobo and pile into the middle of a serving plate.

Mix together the red onion and sweetcorn and stir it through the bean mixture. Drizzle over the dressing, then finish with the coriander and chilli. Taste for seasoning and add more salt and pepper if you think the dish needs it.

SPICY PEPPER, BROCCOLI & AVOCADO RICE BOWL

The colours just jump straight out at you in this dish. The red of the roasted peppers, the green of the longstem broccoli and the cubed avocado, the pure white of the citrus rice... It's like the flavours are right there in glorious technicolour.

YOU WILL NEED

350g longstem broccoli, trimmed

1 recipe quantity of Coriander & Lime Rice (see p.37)

2 ripe Hass avocados, halved, stoned and flesh diced

4 mixed peppers, charred (see p.26), deseeded and sliced

1 red onion, sliced, charred (see p.26) and diced

FOR THE DRESSING

3 tomatoes, charred (see p.26)

1 tablespoon achiote paste

juice of 2 limes

3 tablespoons vegetable oil

4 teaspoons agave syrup or nectar

1 tablespoon chipotles en adobo

sea salt and ground black pepper

First, lightly steam the broccoli until just tender, then refresh under cold running water and drain. Set aside while you make the dressing.

To make the dressing, blitz all the ingredients together in a blender and season with salt and pepper to taste.

Assemble the bowls like a Japanese bento box: divide the rice between 4 bowls – it should make up about a third of each bowl. Top with the avocados, then layer on the cooked broccoli. Make another layer using the peppers and then finally the onion.

Put the dressing in a bowl and place on the table to let everyone help themselves.

BREAKFASTS

BREAKFAST IS ONE OF THE DAYPARTS WE HAVEN'T QUITE MANAGED TO CONQUER YET IN THE RESTAURANTS. NONETHELESS, OVER THE YEARS WE'VE PLAYED AROUND AND COME UP WITH SOME AWESOME DISHES. THIS SEEMS LIKE A GOOD TIME TO INTRODUCE YOU TO THEM. ONCE YOU REALIZE HOW RIGHT THEY ARE, AND IF YOU THINK WE SHOULD START SERVING BREAKFAST, GIVE US A HOLLER AT MARKETING@ CHILANGO.CO.UK WITH THE SUBJECT: "WHEN THE CHORIZO ARE YOU GOING TO DO BREAKFAST?" (THIS SECTION IS NOT ACTUALLY WRITTEN BY ERIC AND WE NEED SUPPORT TO PULL IT OFF. WE ALL *KNOW* BREAKFAST IS A GOOD IDEA.)

BREAKFAST BURRITOS

Breakfast is something the UK does amazingly well, so it would be stupid not to marry Chilango's passion for burritos with the British ability to lay down a good morning spread. This is the best of a British breakfast, Chilango-style.

YOU WILL NEED

4 warmed tortillas

200g Cheddar cheese, grated

½ recipe quantity of Charred Jalapeño Guacamole (see p.56), to serve

½ recipe quantity of Crema de Comal (see p.59)

1 recipe quantity of Roasted Habanero Salsa (see p.51), to serve

FOR THE SPICY BEANS

splash of vegetable oil

4 rashers of streaky smoked bacon

60g black pudding, skin removed and sliced into thin rounds

200g baked beans

½ teaspoon ground cumin

1 teaspoon smoked paprika

1 red jalapeño chilli, charred (see p.26), deseeded and diced

2 tomatoes, charred (see p.26), deseeded and finely chopped

FOR THE SCRAMBLE

4 eggs, lightly beaten

dash of milk, or cream if it's Sunday

15g salted butter

sea salt and ground black pepper

Preheat the oven to 180°C/350°F/Gas 4.

First, make the spicy beans. Heat a little oil in a large frying pan over a medium heat and fry the bacon and black pudding for about 8 minutes, turning once, until golden and crisp. Drain on kitchen paper and set aside.

Put the baked beans, spices, jalapeño and tomatoes in a small saucepan and warm gently over a low heat. Dice the black pudding and bacon and stir them into the beans. Set aside and keep warm.

To make the scramble, season the eggs with salt and pepper, add a dash of milk or cream and beat with a fork until combined. Melt the butter in a small non-stick saucepan over a medium–low heat. Add the egg mixture and turn gently until scrambled. Turn off the heat just before the eggs are ready, so they don't overcook and dry out. Reheat the beans if needed.

To assemble the burritos, divide the spicy beans into 4 equal portions and use each portion to top a warmed tortilla. Add equal amounts of the scrambled egg and Cheddar cheese, then top with a generous dollop of the guacamole and a drizzle of crema. Roll each burrito and serve with the salsa on the side.

HUEVOS RANCHEROS

The "go to" for any Mexican-inspired breakfast, Huevos Rancheros were traditionally served as mid-morning sustenance for farmers, but are now the Mexican equivalent of a full English. This recipe is veggie, a tip we picked up from our north London neighbour, chef Yottam Ottolenghi, who has been making *shakshuku* (a close Middle Eastern equivalent) for years. If you fancy some meat, though, **add some cooked chorizo to the tomato sauce with the black beans and fresh tomatoes.**

YOU WILL NEED

1 tablespoon olive oil

1 small white onion

2 garlic cloves, dry roasted (see p.26)

½ red pepper, deseeded and chopped into bite-sized chunks

400g tin of chopped tomatoes

1 teaspoon agave syrup or nectar

1 teaspoon sea salt

1 teaspoon smoked paprika

1 teaspoon ground cumin

2 red jalapeño chillies, charred (see p.26) and finely chopped

100g tinned black beans, drained and rinsed

200g tomatoes, charred (see p.26), deseeded and chopped

4 eggs

1 Hass avocado, halved, stoned and flesh sliced lengthways

1 handful of coriander leaves, chopped

dried chilli flakes

4 warmed tortillas

sea salt and ground black pepper

Heat the oil in a large heavy-based casserole or ovenproof cast-iron sauté pan over a medium heat. Add the onion, garlic and red pepper and cook for 10 minutes, stirring occasionally, until softened.

Meanwhile, in a blender, purée the tinned tomatoes, agave and salt with 300ml of water, and set aside.

Stir the spices, 1 chopped jalapeño and the tomato mixture into the pan. Bring to the boil, then reduce the heat to low and simmer for 40–45 minutes, uncovered, until the sauce has reduced and thickened. The sauce should be thick enough to make a channel when a spoon is drawn through it. Season with salt and pepper, to taste.

Preheat the oven to 180°C/350°F/Gas 4.

Stir the black beans and fresh tomatoes into the sauce. Make 4 wells in the sauce, then crack 1 egg into each well, keeping the yolks intact. Scatter over the remaining jalapeño and cook in the oven for 10–12 minutes, or until the egg whites are set but the yolks remain runny. Divide between 4 plates and top with equal amounts of the avocado, and a sprinkling of coriander and chilli flakes. Serve with warm tortillas for scooping up the sauce.

MEXICAN OMELETTE

All hail the Mexican breakfast omelette! Think brunchy weekend breakfasts that set you up well for the day ahead. And – best of all – you can use any leftovers for dinner. Two meals for the price of one!

YOU WILL NEED

1 large potato, about 300g, quartered

2 tablespoons olive oil

1 white onion, sliced

1 red pepper, charred (see p.26), deseeded and diced

2 green jalapeño chillies, charred (see p.26) and diced

4 eggs

1 teaspoon sea salt

juice of ½ lime

1 handful of chopped coriander leaves

Crema de Comal, or crema of choice (see pp.58–9)

½ recipe quantity of Pico de Gallo (see p.55)

Boil the potato quarters for 15 minutes, or until tender, then leave until cool enough to handle. Peel off the skin and slice. Set aside.

Preheat the oven to 180°C/350°F/Gas 4.

While the oven is warming, heat the oil in a 20cm ovenproof frying pan over a medium–high heat. Add the onions and fry for 5 minutes, stirring, then add the potatoes and cook for another 5 minutes, until golden and crisp. Add the red pepper and 1 jalapeño and cook for another 2 minutes, until softened slightly.

In a separate bowl, beat the eggs until there are no stringy bits, then mix in the salt and lime juice. Pour the egg mixture over the vegetables in the frying pan and stir gently until evenly distributed. Put the pan in the oven for 10 minutes, or until the omelette is just set and firm.

Remove the pan from the oven, leave the omelette to rest for 5 minutes, then run a round-bladed knife around the edge to loosen. Place a plate on top of the pan and carefully invert the omelette onto the plate. Scatter over the remaining jalapeño and the coriander and serve cut into wedges with your choice of crema and the Pico de Gallo.

PART FOUR

DESSERTS

LIZZY'S DESSERT BURRITOS

Lizzy in Marketing came up with this burrito one lazy Sunday morning when she was faced with some leftover rice and a banana. We're desperately trying to avoid saying "Coconut Rice Arancini" but that's pretty much what this is – in a burrito. This recipe will end your feast with a sugar high. Alternatively, it works as well for breakfast as it does for dessert. Lizzy says: "If you don't care for peanuts feel free to change the peanut butter for a non-nut-based chocolate spread."

YOU WILL NEED

30g unsalted butter

150g arborio risotto rice

225ml coconut milk

pinch of sea salt

½ teaspoon vanilla extract

30g caster sugar, plus extra for sprinkling the bananas

55–70 chocolate nibs or drops

55g plain flour

2 eggs, lightly beaten

55g panko breadcrumbs

vegetable oil, for deep-frying

4 bananas, halved lengthways

4 tablespoons peanut butter or nut-free chocolate spread

4 warmed tortillas

splash of maple syrup

40g unsalted pistachios, roughly chopped

Melt the butter in a saucepan over a medium heat. Add the rice and toast for a couple of minutes. Add the coconut milk, 250ml of water, and the salt, vanilla and sugar, and stir. Lower the heat and simmer for 25–30 minutes, until the rice is cooked slightly softer than normal risotto rice, and sticky. Leave to cool. When cool, form the rice into 14 balls, each roughly the size of a conker or large walnut. Press 4 or 5 chocolate nibs into the centre of each, moulding the rice around the nibs to completely encase them.

Put the flour, eggs and breadcrumbs in separate shallow bowls. Pour enough oil into a large saucepan or deep-fat fryer to deep-fry the arancini. Heat the oil to 185°C/365°F, or until a cube of day-old bread turns crisp and golden in 45 seconds. Heat the oven to low.

Working in batches of 3 or 4 balls at a time, dunk the balls into the flour, then the egg and finally the breadcrumbs until coated. Place straight into the hot oil to deep-fry for 2½–3½ minutes, until golden and crisp. Scoop out the arancini with a slotted spoon and drain on kitchen paper. Repeat, keeping each batch warm in the oven while you fry.

Heat the grill to high. Place the banana halves cut-sides down in a heatproof dish and lightly sprinkle the tops with sugar. Place under the grill until golden and caramelized.

To build the burritos, spread a spoonful of peanut butter or chocolate spread over the middle of each tortilla and drizzle with maple syrup. Add 2 banana halves to each tortilla and 3 or 4 arancini balls. Sprinkle with the pistachios, then wrap and serve. Good luck – it will be messy!

WHY NOT...

Try serving the arancini without the burritos (or bananas) and instead plate them up and serve with a generous drizzling of Chilli-Chocolate Sauce (see p.179), toasted chopped hazelnuts and a spoonful of dulce de leche.

SERVES 4-6

CARNIVAL FRUIT SKEWERS

The sweetness of this dessert at the end of a Mexican feast will help cool down the spicier dishes it follows. However, if things are really hot early on, forget the skewers and serve it as a salad to accompany your burrito and provide immediate cooling refuge for your taste buds.

YOU WILL NEED

1 ripe small pineapple, skin removed,
    flesh cut into 2cm-thick slices and
    charred (see p.26)
1 large ripe mango, peeled, stone
    removed, flesh thickly sliced and
    charred (see p.26)
1 banana
1 ripe papaya, halved, deseeded
    and cut into 2cm chunks
mint leaves, to serve
mixed seeds, to serve

**FOR THE PINEAPPLE, CUMIN
    & CHILLI DRESSING**

2 tablespoons orange juice
1 tablespoon lime juice
½ red bird's eye chilli, deseeded and
    roughly chopped
large pinch of sea salt
¼ teaspoon cumin seeds, toasted
    (see p.26)
large pinch of ground black pepper

Set aside 100g of the pineapple and 50g of the mango after charring (you'll need this to make the dressing). To make the fruit salad, cut the remaining pineapple (discarding the core) and mango into 2cm chunks. Cut the banana at an angle into 2cm-thick slices. Using equal amounts of each fruit (including the papaya) for each skewer, thread the fruit pieces onto 4 to 6 skewers, then set aside while you make the dressing.

To make the dressing, put the reserved pineapple and mango in a blender with the rest of the dressing ingredients and blend until smooth. Spoon the dressing over the fruit skewers – you may have some left over for the same again tomorrow. To serve, sprinkle with the mint leaves and mixed seeds.

S'MURROS WITH CHILLI-CHOCOLATE SAUCE

This recipe takes me back to childhood. Camping in the woods. Sitting fireside. Melting the marshmallows we had hastily speared onto the ends of our wooden sticks, before sandwiching the gooey mess between two graham crackers and a square of chocolate. This is indulgent. And you're gonna love it.

YOU WILL NEED

185g plain flour

½ teaspoon ground cinnamon

20g light brown soft sugar

1 tablespoon vegetable oil

½ teaspoon sea salt

4 eggs

vegetable oil, for deep-frying

at least 8 large marshmallows

CACAO SUGAR

20g caster sugar

1 teaspoon cacao powder

½ teaspoon ground cinnamon

FOR THE CHILLI-CHOCOLATE SAUCE

100g 70% dark chocolate

100ml double cream

pinch of ground ancho chilli

pinch of ground chipotle chilli

Make a dough. Sift together the flour and cinnamon in a bowl. Put 210ml of water, along with the sugar, vegetable oil and salt in a saucepan and bring to the boil over a medium heat. Reduce the heat to low, add the flour mixture and stir quickly with a wooden spoon to a rough dough. Put the dough in a mixer with the paddle attachment. Add the eggs, 1 at a time, and beat on medium to make a smooth, loose dough. Alternatively, do this in a bowl and beat well with a wooden spoon.

Line 2 baking trays with baking paper. Spoon the dough into a piping bag with a 1cm star nozzle. Pipe the dough into at least 16 4cm-diameter spirals (start at the centre of each spiral and work outwards) on the baking trays. Freeze for about 15 minutes to firm up.

Meanwhile, mix together all the ingredients for the cacao sugar in a shallow bowl and set aside.

Make the chilli-chocolate sauce. Melt the chocolate in a heatproof bowl set over a saucepan of simmering water, making sure the bowl doesn't touch the water. When the chocolate has melted, carefully remove the bowl from the heat. Stir in the cream and the ground ancho and chipotle. Set aside.

Pour enough oil into a large, deep saucepan or deep-fat fryer to deep-fry the churros. Heat the oil to 185°C/365°F, or until a cube of day-old bread turns crisp and golden in 45 seconds. Working in batches of 4, deep-fry the churros for 4–6 minutes, until golden and crisp. Scoop out each batch with a slotted spoon and drain on kitchen paper while you cook the next.

Put the marshmallows on a heatproof surface and, working in batches, toast with a blow torch and soften them enough to stick (you could heat them briefly in a microwave – about 10 seconds on full power). To make the s'murros, turn half of the cooked churros flat-side up. Top each with a softened marshmallow, then place another churro on top, flat-side down and press lightly to sandwich. Sprinkle with the cacao sugar and serve with the chilli-chocolate sauce for dunking.

THIS PAGE: **CARNIVAL FRUIT SKEWERS (P.178)** OPPOSITE (TOP):
S'MURROS WITH CHILLI-CHOCOLATE SAUCE (P.179)
OPPOSITE (BOTTOM): **SMOKY FRUIT SALSA EMPANADAS (P.182)**

SMOKY FRUIT SALSA EMPANADAS

These will be delicious at any point in the year, but this year skip the Christmas pudding and have these instead. Frying the empanadas is definitely best, but – we get it – baking is healthier, so we've given you both cooking instructions. The filling is out-of-this-world. Your guests will love you – take a bow.

YOU WILL NEED

325g plain flour, plus extra for
    dusting
1 teaspoon sea salt
60g cold unsalted butter, cut into
    small pieces
1 egg (plus 1 extra if baking)
1½ teaspoons white wine vinegar
vegetable oil, for deep-frying
    (optional)
dulce de leche, to serve

FOR THE FILLING

40g unsalted butter
1 small ripe mango, stone removed,
    flesh sliced and charred (see p.26)
250g pineapple, skin and core
    removed, flesh cubed and charred
    (see p.26)
1 large banana, sliced
1 red bird's eye chilli, deseeded and
    diced
2 tablespoons orange juice
finely grated zest of ½ unwaxed
    orange
pinch of sea salt
3 tablespoons runny honey
½ teaspoon ground allspice
pinch of ground nutmeg

To make the empanada dough, sift the flour and salt into a mixing bowl. Rub in the butter with your fingertips until it resembles coarse breadcrumbs. In a separate bowl, beat together the egg and vinegar with 70ml of water. Stir the egg mixture into the flour mixture with a fork until you have a loose dough. Turn out onto a floured work surface and knead it to bring the dough together into a ball. Take care not to overwork the dough or get it too warm. Press the dough out into a 1cm-thick rectangle, wrap it in cling film and leave it to rest in the fridge for at least 1 hour.

Meanwhile, make the filling. Melt the butter in a large frying pan over a medium–low heat. Add the mango, pineapple and banana and cook gently until softened. Add the chilli, orange juice and zest, salt and honey and cook to a thick syrup. Stir in the spices. Remove from the heat and leave to cool.

Line a large baking tray with baking paper. Remove the dough from the fridge. Dust a work surface with flour and roll out the dough to about 3mm thick. Using a 20cm cutter, stamp out 4 rounds of dough. Add 2 tablespoons of the fruit filling mixture to the middle of each round, brush the edge with water and fold one half of the dough over the filling to make a pasty shape. Crimp the edges to seal and place the empanadas on the lined baking tray. Chill for 30 minutes.

To deep-fry, pour enough oil into a large deep saucepan or deep-fat fryer. Heat the oil to 185°C/365°F, or until a cube of day-old bread turns crisp and golden in 45 seconds. Deep-fry the chilled empanadas in 2 batches for 4–6 minutes each, or until golden and crisp. Scoop out each batch with a slotted spoon and drain on kitchen paper.

To bake the empanadas, preheat the oven to 180°C/350°F/Gas 4. Lightly beat a second egg in a bowl (you won't need this egg if you're frying). Brush the tops with the egg and bake for 25–30 minutes, until golden. Transfer to a wire rack to cool slightly before serving.

Serve the empanadas with dulce de leche.

SERVES
4

CHILLI-CHOCOLATE FONDANTS

The world will never agree whether this is eaten with thick, creamy vanilla ice cream or fresh double cream. And there's no space to settle it in one paragraph, so debate it among yourselves.

YOU WILL NEED

100g unsalted butter, plus extra for greasing

100g 70% dark chocolate, broken into pieces

1 Scotch bonnet chilli, deseeded and finely diced

100g plain flour

pinch of sea salt

2 eggs, lightly beaten

2 egg yolks

100g caster sugar

½ recipe quantity of Ancho & Cacao Salt (see p.149)

thick double cream or vanilla ice cream

Preheat the oven to 160°C/315°F/Gas 2–3. Grease 4 fondant pudding moulds or large ramekins with butter.

Gently melt the butter and chocolate with the chilli in a heatproof bowl set over a saucepan of gently simmering water, making sure the bottom of the bowl doesn't touch the water. When the chocolate has melted, carefully remove the bowl from the heat and leave the mixture to cool slightly.

Sift together the flour and salt into a bowl.

Whisk the eggs, yolks and sugar in a separate mixing bowl until pale and creamy, about 2 minutes. Gradually, pour in the chocolate mixture, whisking continuously, then fold in the flour mixture.

Divide the pudding batter between the 4 moulds or ramekins. Bake for 12–14 minutes, until the fondants have risen, but are still runny in the middle. Turn out and serve with a sprinkling of the Ancho & Cacao Salt and with cream or ice cream by the side.

HIBISCUS POLENTA CAKE

We wolfed down plenty of desserts made using masa harina (a type of corn flour) during our ramblings through Mexico. However, masa harina is not easily available in the UK, so we're bringing you this deliciousness using polenta instead. Oh, and homemade hibiscus syrup is going to become your cordial of choice from now on. Traditionally used to make *agua fresca*, this tart, fresh and bright red drink is a staple of Mexican street fare and adds another dimension to your polenta cake.

YOU WILL NEED

200g unsalted butter, plus extra for greasing

200g caster sugar

4 eggs, lightly beaten

finely grated zest of 3 unwaxed lemons

100g ground almonds

200g fine polenta

2 teaspoons baking powder

small handful of roughly chopped pistachios (optional), to serve

FOR THE HIBISCUS SYRUP

juice of 3 lemons, about 80ml

75g caster sugar

10g dried hibiscus flowers

Preheat the oven to 160°C/315°F/Gas 2–3. Line the base and grease the sides of a 20cm-square baking tin.

Beat the butter and sugar together in a mixing bowl until pale and creamy. Beat in the eggs, one at a time (don't worry if the mixture curdles a bit), then fold in the lemon zest.

Mix together the ground almonds, polenta and baking powder, then fold the dry ingredients into the wet in 3 batches. Pour the batter into the prepared cake tin – don't forget to lick the bowl (with caveats about the raw egg, of course). Bake for 50–55 minutes, or until golden and risen and a skewer inserted into the centre comes out clean. Leave the cake to stand in the tin for 10 minutes, then transfer to a wire rack to cool completely.

To make the hibiscus syrup, put the lemon juice, sugar and hibiscus flowers in a small saucepan and heat gently, stirring until the sugar dissolves and it turns syrupy and vibrant pink in colour.

Puncture the cake all over with a skewer and pour the syrup over so it seeps into the cake. Serve in squares sprinkled with pistachios (if using) and with any leftover syrup on the side.

LEFT: **HIBISCUS POLENTA CAKE**
RIGHT: **CHILLI-CHOCOLATE FONDANTS (P.183)**

THE BIG BURRITO TASTING TABLE

If today is Monday and yesterday you've splashed out on Chicken 14 with all the trimmings, you may end up with some leftover salsa and not know what to do with it. This chart has the answer. All the extras are shown legibly down the side. If you want to read the main recipes without getting a crick in your neck, you'll have to turn the book by 90°.

CHICKEN

Section	Item	CHILANGO CHICKEN (P.74)	CHICKEN FAJITAS (P.76)	CHICKEN TINGA (P.77)	PUEBLA CHICKEN MOLE (P.80)	YUCATÁN ACHIOTE MARINATED CHICKEN (P.81)	CHILANGO FRIED CHICKEN (P.82)	ONE-PAN ROASTED TOMATILLO CHICKEN (P.84)	CHARGRILLED JALAPEÑO CHICKEN (P.85)	CHICKEN BIRYANI (P.88)	VIETNAMESE LEMONGRASS CHICKEN (P.89)	CHICKEN AL PASTOR-STYLE (P.90)	BBQ CHIPOTLE CHICKEN (P.91)	CHICKEN 14 (P.96)
RICE & BEANS	SPICY CHILLI RICE (P.36)													
	CORIANDER & LIME RICE (P.37)	●		●	●	●		●					●	●
	ARROZ MEXICANA (P.37)											●		
	ARROZ VERDE (P.40)						●							
	CARAMELIZED COCONUT RICE (P.41)									●	●			
	MEXICAN QUINOA (P.42)													
	CHARRO BEANS (P.46)				●			●				●		
	CHIPOTLE BLACK BEANS (P.47)	●				●								
SALSAS, GUACS & CREMAS	SMOKY CORN SALSA (P.50)									●				
	ROASTED PINEAPPLE SALSA (P.50)		●		●									
	ROASTED HABANERO SALSA (P.51)						●		●					●
	SMOKY TOMATO SALSA (P.51)	●												
	TOMATILLO & AVOCADO SALSA (P.54)							●						
	RED TAQUERÍA SALSA (P.54)													
	PICO DE GALLO (P.55)	●			●				●					
	SALSA VERDE (P.55)			●										
	CLASSIC GUACAMOLE (P.56)		●										●	
	CHARRED PINEAPPLE WITH QUICK PICKLED JALAPEÑOS (P.153)									●	●			
	CHARRED JALAPEÑO GUACAMOLE (P.56)					●			●					
	CHIPOTLE CREMA (P.58)	●											●	
	LIME & JALAPEÑO CREMA (P.58)										●			
	CREMA DE COMAL (P.59)								●					
	ROASTED GARLIC CREMA (P.59)		●	●			●						●	
SLAWS	BAJA CABBAGE SLAW (P.64)						●		●					
	SHREDDED LETTUCE						●							
TOPPERS	PICKLED ONION			●					●					
	CORIANDER LEAVES			●	●				●		●		●	●
	SLICED RED JALAPEÑO						●							
	SLICED CHARRED GREEN JALAPEÑO		●						●					
	CHEDDAR CHEESE			●				●				●		

	BEEF							PORK							FISH & SEAFOOD						VEGGIE			

BEEF
- BBQ BRAISED BEEF BRISKET (P.101)
- BARBACOA BEEF (P.102)
- STEAK FAJITAS (P.103)
- BRAISED SHORT RIBS (P.106)
- CHIMICHURRI STEAK (P.107)
- CHARGRILLED THAI STEAK WITH PINEAPPLE SALSA (P.108)
- GRILLED STEAK TAMPIQUEÑA (P.112)

PORK
- CARNE ASADA (P.113)
- STICKY CHORIZO (P.118)
- PORK MONDONGO (P.119)
- SLOW-COOKED BBQ PULLED PORK (P.122)
- PORK CARNITAS (P.123)
- PORCHETTA (P.124)
- PORK PIBIL (P.126)

FISH & SEAFOOD
- MACKEREL ESCABECHE (P.134)
- PRAWNS WITH CHORIZO (P.135)
- CAMARÓN ROJO (P.138)
- BAJA FISH TACOS (P.139)
- CHIPOTLE SALMON TACOS (P.142)
- LOBSTER IN BASIL & CHIPOTLE BUTTER TACOS (P.143)

VEGGIE
- PULLED OYSTER MUSHROOMS (P.148)
- ACHIOTE BAKED AUBERGINES (P.149)
- CHARRED PINEAPPLE WITH QUICK PICKLED JALAPEÑOS (P.153)
- MEXICAN BBQ PULLED CELERIAC (P.156)

INDEX

STOCKISTS

Look at how amazing we are listing every single place in the world to buy ingredients. Nah! None of that shit. We've made things easy for you. You can find pretty much everything you need either at your local supermarket or online.

Amazon.co.uk Do we even need to say anything?

Mexgrocer.co.uk These guys have their own section on Amazon and have got a great range of ingredients online – a great one-stop shop for pretty much all that's in this book.

Brindisa To call this a Spanish deli is to massively undersell this amazing food store (if you're in London, use it online at brindisa.com if you're not). The chorizo (and so much else) is to die for.

The Cool Chile Company Oh, we do like these guys! An honest and approachable company with a stall at Borough Market in London selling fresh tortilla chips. Also one of the few channels through which you can actually buy fresh tomatillos online.

ACKNOWLEDGEMENTS

Our guests and fans. You've paid the bills over the last 10 years. Without your passionate following, there would be no business, no Chilango, no book. Many of you have not only invested your lunches and dinners with us, but also your hard-earned cash, as an investor through one of our many crowdfunding campaigns. Thanks for helping us build Chilango, the offspring of which is the very book you're reading.

Our amazing restaurant, support, and supplier teams. A very special mention goes to Luis Castro. You built the foundation upon which our food sits to this day, and to James Robins and Nuno Mendes, for helping us take things up a level and continuously improve. Eating, cooking and working at Chilango since 2007 has never felt like a "job" because of the amazing people that have come together, past and present, to make our outfit what it is today. This book is not the culmination of just a few months, but the result of a decade of grafting. Thanks for helping us add flavour to people's lives, each and every day. You all represent the vibrancy that our brand stands for. Keep on shining. Thank you.

Mark Miller. Where do I begin. Sensei? Yoda? Zen Master? I remember calling you back in July 2017. "We've been asked to do a cookbook. What do you think? Should we do it?" Thanks for your guidance and for helping us create and source the myriad recipes that feature throughout the book. While our guests and teams got us up to this point, we could only start the cookbook marathon because of your truly invaluable support. And for all the rest of ya, Mark has been a friend and advisor to Chilango for 10 years. He's also the author of over 12 cookbooks of his own. Look him up on Amazon. Your taste buds will salute you.

Stefan Cosser & Dan Booth, along with the other dudes in Waterloo, for helping us craft, produce and tweak the recipes. It was a thrilling ride that left me nearly bursting following some of our tasting sessions. Mustn't eat too much during the first half of the session. I never learn. Hats off to you all.

Jude, Manisha & Nicky: Alchemists. The three of you. Turning our scraps of twisted iron and steel into gold, to render the beautiful book we now have in our hands. We are great at running restaurants, but book-making is a different kettle of fish. Thanks for guiding us and for cracking the whip, as well as reducing the number of fucks and shits in the text. At least we managed to sneak two more into the final pages.

Dave & Becci: Five long, long days in Chilango Towers for the photoshoot. You guys knocked it out of the park, though. We've never been more proud of the way our food looked since you touched our recipes. All of us were scared shitless that a book on burritos was going to look like a catalogue of tinfoil turds; you've proven otherwise.

Last but not least, the Dutchman. Danny de Ruiter. You busted out some true project management wizardry to create this book. I was super-impressed with your ability to break down large amounts of information and complex tasks, while making sure we delivered something amazing in the end. You fucking rock and, at the end of the day, you literally made the book happen, and got it across the line. Thank you, from here to the Kop van Zuid and back.

I might have forgotten somebody. If so, it wasn't intentional.